D0065796

# JANÁČEK

## LEAVES FROM HIS LIFE

Edited and translated by

Vilem and Margaret Tausky

KAHN & AVERILL, LONDON

*To the memory of Margaret Tausky*

First published in 1982 by Stanmore Press Ltd
under their associated imprint: Kahn & Averill

British Library Cataloguing in Publication Data

Janacek, Leos
  Leoš, Janáček.
  1. Janacek, Leos    2. Composers—Czechoslavakia
  —Biography
  I. Title
  780'.92'4     ML410.J18

ISBN 0-900707-68-2

Printed in Great Britain by
The Thetford Press Ltd, Thetford, Norfolk

# CONTENTS

## Illustrations

# RECOLLECTIONS
# OF LEOŠ JANÁČEK

## by Vilem Tausky

Leoš Janáček was a great creative personality belonging not only to Czech music, but also to the musical literature of the world. With his originality he enriched and revolutionised the musical scene of his time.

In the fifty years of my life as a professional musician, undoubtedly the greatest single influence on my work has been that of Leoš Janáček. When I entered the Janáček Conservatoire at the age of seventeen, I already had some inkling of the new ideas in music which he was promoting.

But what a privilege to have learnt under his direction! Not only as a musician, but as a man, for his interests in life covered a wide field.

Unfortunately he died before I left the Conservatoire, but not before I had grasped the new ideals in music for which he stood, and I was fortunate to work with a staff of professors, all of whom were his own pupils and dedicated to developing the principles he had laid down.

Firstly, I should like to recount the impression he made on me, and then to speak of him as I learnt to know him through our teachers, his devoted pupils.

In the beginning it seemed that his was just a continuation of the traditional Czech music of Dvořák and Smetana, music which he admired tremendously. But very soon, from the strength of his own personality, he created a style which was entirely his own, and which was to influence the music of the composers of the 20th century.

If we think of Janáček's work as a constant and uncompromising growth in thought and ideas and of his opposition to the social and cultural life at the end of the 19th century, we shall easily understand what a fight he had to undertake for any recognition.

We could divide his growing artistic individuality into three periods. During his early youth and sojourn in the cloister where he trained as a teacher, he was mainly under the influence of Czech national music. From this time come the operas, *Šárka*, and the *Beginning of a Novel*.

The second period would be until the end of the First World War in 1918, when Czechoslovakia emerged as an independent country. During these years he became very critical of the decadence of verismus and the beginning of a disintegration of musical composition in Western Europe. It was then that he successfully built his new approach to the hard realism of life. His background was that of a poor teacher's family and he spent his youth among country people, and although it was a beautiful country, it was socially and economically oppressed. It is from these circumstances that we must look for the roots of his music, and learn to understand his tragic and dark musical ideas.

The whole of his life's work reflects his nation's centuries-old struggle for material freedom and a cultural identity. From these days stems also his immersion in folk music. His romantic love for the country, and the rough realism of the Lachian people is perfectly mirrored in his music. On one side the highly romantic inspiration of love with typical Janáček lyrical melodies, and in contrast the wildly explosive realism expressed in his crude harmonic and orchestral outbursts.

All his inspiration came from the music of the people, and

he was the first after Smetana and Dvořák to transmute this music into his own idiom. No wonder that when *Jenufa* (1896-1904) appeared in this completely new idiom it failed to gain understanding when it was measured by the operas of the western world of that time. He had to wait until 1916 in Prague, and 1918 in Vienna, for the musical world to become aware of a masterpiece. From this period came also his great collection of folk-songs. He said: ''The composer is a human being: the deeper his experience, the better his expression of it. The composer must be concerned with nature and society. There are composers who don't care about what goes on around them. They write at the table. And one of their compositions is the same as another.'' This is why in all his operas he depicted people as he knew them.

The stresses under which he himself worked during the writing of *Jenufa*, especially in the latter half, are revealed in a letter which he wrote to his friend, Nebuška, in 1917. ''I started to compose *Jenufa* in 1896. For me, in those days, time to compose was stolen time! To be choirmaster and organist, music teacher at the Teachers' Training College, director of the Organ School, conductor of the concerts of the Philharmonic Society, and to have a dying child at home — that was my life! Certainly it was difficult to compose, and therefore it came slowly, and I remember it with a heavy heart.'' The dying child was his beloved daughter, Olga, who died in 1903. A few days before she died, ''Daddy, play me your opera'', she said, for she knew she would never hear a performance, and she listened with enjoyment. Janáček himself said that *Jenufa* should be bound with a black ribbon of mourning for his daughter, Olga, and his little son, Vladimir, and he added to the title page ''to the memory of my daughter, Olga''.

Finally, the third period of his work, and undoubtedly the greatest, was from 1918 until his death in 1928.

Janáček at the age of about fifty

Encouraged by the political and social development of his beloved country, and by the recognition given to *Jenufa* on its production in Vienna in 1918, he feverishly wrote his greatest works in the last ten years of his life. The following compositions date from this period:

| | |
|---|---|
| Katia Kabanová | 1919-21 |
| The Cunning Little Vixen | 1921-23 |
| The Macropulos Affair | 1923-25 |
| House of the Dead | 1927-28 |
| Glagolithic Mass | 1926 |
| Taras Bulba | 1918 |
| Ballad of Blaník | 1920 |
| Sinfonietta | 1926 |
| Danube (unfinished) | 1928 |
| Concertino for Piano | 1925 |
| Capriccio | 1926 |
| String Quartet No.1 | |
| (Kreutzer Sonata) | 1923- 4 |
| Wind Quintet Mládí | 1924 |
| String Quartet No.2. | |
| (Intimate Letters) | 1928 |

The Organ School that he founded in his home town, grew from nine scholars into the Brno Conservatoire with 186 pupils, which opened in 1918, and was largely due to his efforts. This was also a source of inspiration to him. In fact, it would be difficult to say whether his contribution to the world of music was greater in the field of teaching or of composition. It was not only his own teaching, but his wisdom in securing talented young composers as the professors at Brno Conservatoire. They were musicians who were thoroughly imbued with his original principles.

After his death these men were determined to advance the work he had begun, in the true Janáček spirit. František

Neumann, the director of the Brno Opera taught conducting at the Conservatoire; Oswald Chlubna, one of Janáček's closest associates, was a teacher of Instrumentation and a composer. After Janáček's death he wrote the final 17 bars of the *House of the Dead*. Then there was Jaroslav Kvapil, pianist and composer, who conducted the first performance of the *Glagolithic Mass*. Another gifted teacher of composition who taught me was Vilém Petrželka. These, and many others, inspired by Janáček's example, carried his enlightenment into their teaching and their performances.

Although *Jenufa* did not meet with general understanding at the first performance, Janáček's pupils were wildly enthusiastic about it. Kaprál, a student at the Organ School, and later a professor there, remembered

### Jenufa 1904 — Brno Performance

We students sat in the gallery and eagerly followed the performance. The enthusiasm was enormous. Janáček was thunderously called, over and over again, and was honoured with laurel wreaths. After the performance he was carried by the soloists, still in their costumes, to the Assembly Rooms. The dramatic effect of the work was indisputably great. Musically, the work impressed us by its utterly new idiom and divided us young listeners into passionate followers, or adversaries, of this utterly new expression. We must not forget that the artistic measure of that period was the works of Wagner; from that point of view the people who judged could hardly be expected to have any taste for a completely opposite musical idiom.

We Janáčekians were naturally immediately enthused by the true and lively expression, while the Wagnerians were boasting of the grandiloquence of Wagner's music, quoting as an example the 'Wedding March' from *Lohengrin*, which cannot be compared with the wedding scene at the end of Janáček's opera. We didn't give in, and we proved to the Wagnerians that the situation in Janáček's opera is completely different and therefore requires music of a different character.

After the 1918 Revolution, the Brno Theatre became a Czech National Theatre, and on Janáček's initiative František Neumann was made director of the new Opera House. During the ten years of his reign, he worked steadily and conscientiously in the direction of the new spirit, and under his and Janáček's influence the Brno Opera gained international recognition.

Janáček pointed out another weakness in Brno's musical life. There were no regular symphony concerts, because the city could not support its own symphony orchestra, so Janáček made provision in the contract of the musical director of the Opera House that he should include regular symphony concerts during the run of the theatre season. This ruling of course had an influence on the quality of the orchestral players. They had a chance to display their artistry apart from accompanying operas and operettas, and through these concerts he gave an opportunity for a whole generation of young Moravian composers to receive a hearing. In this way Janáček built around the theatre a circle of composers, who, through the inspired conducting of Neumann, became an artistic community, called The Club of Moravian Composers.

For as long as he lived, Neumann conducted all the first performances of Janáček's operas. Inevitably at times tensions arose. Oswald Chlubna, who was my professor of orchestration, used to tell a rather typical Janáček story. "Janáček said 'I have heard my works performed on stages all over the world, but I must say that Neumann still gives the best performances.' " Surely this was the greatest acknowledgment that Janáček ever made. He held in special love and esteem people who understood and admired his work. He always talked in this way about director Neumann, the producer Zítek, Professor Kudláček, the leader of the orchestra, Kvapil, the conductor, and others. But still a dissonance sometimes crept into this harmony, but only temporarily.

Shortly before the première of *Katia Kabanová*, Neumann threw the score on the floor, in disgust at the many mistakes. Janáček, without a word, quietly picked it up, took it home, and during the night corrected all the mistakes that the not very conscientious copyist had made. Janáček never talked about that episode; only to me he quietly sighed ''At the beginning I couldn't recognise it, so many mistakes. But you listen now — how it sounds! Wonderful! Let us speak no more about it!'' Today we can say with conviction that Janáček made Neumann, and Neumann made Janáček, and that the Brno National Opera House was the gateway through which Janáček's works went out into the world, and the beginning of his world-wide recognition.

Janáček was still working on the tragic opera *Katia Kabanová* when he found the subject for his next opera. The *Lidové Noviny* (Brno newspaper) to which he sometimes contributed articles, more regularly after 1919, brought his attention to a long story in their literary supplement, *The Little Vixen* by Rudolf Těsnohlídek.

From then on during the period 1921-23 his full creative energies were given to the composition of *The Little Vixen*. The writer, Těsnohlídek, could hardly believe in Janáček's interest in such a subject, and wrote charmingly about their first meeting:

> The little vixen played her tricks in the newspapers. I don't know why she is so popular, probably because she is of the earth, earthy.
>
> I had no idea that she had an eager reader and admirer in a man with silvery hair and sparkling eyes. I knew him only from a distance because he is a musician, and I know nothing about music. Suddenly I heard that she had bewitched him and that he wants to express her often trivial speech and her even more often trivial actions, in music, which is the least earthy of the arts.
>
> I didn't believe it; I thought it was a joke. Then I received a

direct enquiry as to what I thought of the idea. I didn't say anything. I was so surprised, and I felt that someone was making a fool of me, until one spring day a couple of years ago when I had a written invitation from Mistr Janáček.

My heart was heavier than Bystrouška's when she was caught in the larder, eating pork, but I summoned up courage and went. It was a May day, and the bird songs sounded high above the Brno streets, over the roofs, and under the sky, as if it were somewhere like the meadows by the River Svitava.

Leoš Janáček awaited me in the Conservatoire garden. He sat under the hedges, thousands of tiny little white blossoms above his head, and his head, equally white, seemed to me to be the biggest blossom of them all. He smiled and I knew at once that it was the smile that creates life, like the golden decoration for courage before the enemy. Heroism in the face of grief, humiliation and rage. At that moment I believed that the little vixen gets tamed and subjugated by the kindness of people in a little garden, and that unseen she comes to settle at our feet, and listens to our intrigues. Janáček volunteered a few words about the story, and then he started talking about *his* forest in Valachia, which I don't know at all. He talked about his studies of the twittering of birds, and I saw that he understood the power of a smile.

And after the premières? Janáček never omitted to thank his collaborators one and all, without particularising.

Showing how he valued this collaboration there is a letter preserved in the archives of the orchestra, after the famous première of *The Macropulos Affair*:

To the Orchestra of the National Theatre in Brno.

Honoured gentlemen,

During the first rehearsals I crawled through the corridors of the theatre, like Jeremiah under the ruins of Jerusalem. I was sweating in fear that you won't be able to do it, and that I haven't done it myself. We passed each other speechlessly.

And yet you did it magnificently under Neumann's baton — and so after all I did it too!

Thank you from my heart for the achievement!

Your devoted

Ph. Dr. Leoš Janáček

The year 1924 was a rather memorable one which Neumann wanted to celebrate by means of a symphony concert. The centenary of Smetana's birth, the seventieth birthday of Janáček and the fiftieth birthday of Josef Suk fell in that year, so Neumann planned a programme containing works by all three of them, but not announcing any reason for this. The concert was fixed for January 13th 1924. As well as Suk's symphony *The Ripening*, Janáček's *Taras Bulba* was included.

Janáček, as usual, went eagerly to all the rehearsals, explained, made the necessary corrections, and was very much looking forward to the performance, but had no idea that it was to be a celebration of his 70th birthday. When he saw the theatre programme, the secret was out!

The Manager of the orchestra, Habrda, tells what happened:

> On the day of the concert we saw Janáček, as usual, walking about in the upper circle, his favourite part of the house. After the performance the composer was, as customary, to take a bow on the stage and thank the audience for the wonderful reception. They called for him in vain. In the end director Neumann had to stop the unending applause with the announcement that the composer had disappeared from the theatre and was nowhere to be found.

> He really had disappeared, and the reason for his exit was given next day in a letter to the orchestra:

> Honoured gentlemen,

> Through an unfortunate accident I was not with you when, through your strenous efforts, my *Taras Bulba* came to life.

> But to celebrate my seventieth birthday, when I have not yet reached it, I don't understand, I am not going to give away one minute of my life, and I am sure that not one of you would yield

one minute of yours either, and surely none of you would wish to take from me even a moment, especially now when it is so lovely to live in our new republic.

So don't hold it against me that my thanks come in writing. To you all and to the conductor, director Neumann in particular — Congratulations!

Yours devotedly,

Leoš Janáček

Brno, January 14th 1924

**Vilém Petrželka, who was my Professor of Composition, recalled for us one particular lesson with the Master:**

I remember one memorable hour of composition with Leoš Janáček in 1907. The Master explained the difference between operatic overtures of the past and the short introduction to a modern opera, and said, 'Today I have brought as an example the introduction to my opera, *Jenufa*. It is still at the printers, and I brought this copy from the press.'

Then he started to analyse the beginning of the first act, and we listened with bated breath both to the music and to the ardent words of the Master about his work. Quite clearly it was new music; music which we had never and nowhere heard before. Janáček our director, vanished as in a mist, and before our eyes appeared a great composer writing music of the future. The last words of the Master were:

'*Jenufa* is being printed and will be brought to life. I think that its musical and dramatic truth will find acceptance, and will live in the years ahead. You are young, and so I say to you 'Go with truth, as in life, so in art'.

The Master went, the lesson was finished, the first of that kind which he had given us. It was an hour so full of joy that I shall never forget it.

**Chlubna often told us that Janáček was not always confident of success.**

I wouldn't wish anyone to endure the mood into which he sank when he suffered these doubts. He felt that he was only a little man, with a soul filled with terror. He, who had such inborn dramatic vision, doubted, and waited for public approval.

Everything was dramatically analysed, to the last little detail, composed in Janáček's style, with no unnecessary embellishments, so that I, even at the dress rehearsals, was sure of success, but he seldom counted on it. Only during the performance he began to take heart, and became calmer and surer of his work. It was only when he felt the sympathy of the audience that he grew more confident.

The same lack of confidence showed when he received invitations from abroad. When he was asked to visit the Music Festival in Frankfurt in 1925, in which his *Concertino* was being performed, he was reluctant to go. However, having secured the promises of Professor Kudláček and Professor Krtička, the clarinetist, to go with him, he finally decided to accept the invitation.

The following story was delightfully recounted by Professor Kudláček, the leader of the opera orchestra, and of the Moravian String Quartet:

I often welcomed Janáček to my classroom No.8 at the Minorit Cloister. After my lessons he sometimes played me his new works, and asked for my advice if this or that could be written for a certain instrument, and if it were easily playable.

In this classroom the piano rang out under his strong fingers when he played for me the score of his recently finished string quartet, *Intimate Letters*. His temperamental playing on the piano was so vigorous that he drew blood from his hand, hitting it on one of the keys. Eagerness and effort to find the right interpretation of the ingenious ideas prevented him from noticing the wound until the blood on the keys drew his attention to it. Anybody who knew his unrestrained temperament will believe my story, remembering his special love for this work.

During one of the evening visits to the Cloister, Janáček declared abruptly: ''Here, have 1400 crowns which I extorted from the Ministry for the journey to Frankfurt, and you will come with me to Frankfurt to play my *Concertino* with Ilonka Kurzová (the pianist). We must have somebody there who knows it; the people over there couldn't play it with just one rehearsal''.

So I went, and with me my colleague, the clarinet player, Krtička, whom Janáček took as well to produce a surer performance. As there was a musical exhibition at the Festival, Janáček also obtained permission from the Ministry for his favourite band from Myjava to play at the exhibition in national dress.

In Frankfurt there was only one rehearsal for the *Concertino*, arranged on the morning of the concert, because the members of the theatre orchestra could not be released from the rehearsals for the Festival. Janácek, himself, was present at the rehearsal, as was Dr. Václav Stepán Ilonka's husband. The rehearsal was very tempestuous, because the members of the orchestra were very tired from constant rehearsing for the festival, and showed no interest in serious study. They evidently underestimated Janáček's work, and not realising the particular requirements from each player, thought it would be enough to play it through once. The parts, at which they gave a cursory glance, didn't tell them much; they seemed quite simple, so the players felt quite confident.

We started to rehearse. The viola player sat relaxed next to me, legs crossed, cigarette dangling; he smoked, and occasionally played something — the others, similarly. After the first few bars Janáček jumped up and ran over to the unfortunate viola player: "Hey, my dear sir, what do you think you are playing?" — he stamped, shouted and sang, showing the way it should by played, and the stupified viola player, by constantly repeating the typical Janáček figures, managed to understand this completely unknown idiom, so that in the end his cigarette fell out of his mouth, and he lost all inclination to smoke.

Staring in amazement, his colleagues watched this scene, and I expected now that it would come to an embarrassing and stormy exchange of views. However, the German colleagues, as I noticed later in the rehearsal, were excellent artists, and with their musicianly instinct they recognised that they were playing for a composer of distinction.

Dr. Štěpán took the opportunity, quietly and realistically, to tell them about Janáček and his work. He, himself, took over the rehearsal as I, only a youngster at the time, didn't dare to correct the German colleagues. After further peaceful rehearsing, Dr. Štěpán showed such a detailed knowledge of Janáček's work and exceptional musicality that the rehearsal became a pleasure.

The German colleagues, led now by an experienced hand and enchanted by the beautiful and precise playing of Ilonka, realised that they were playing something both new and great, and continued to rehearse ardently.

The programme in the evening contained Casella and other modern composers. All the composers represented were in the wings, impatiently shifting from one foot to the other, ready to take the stage for a bow. Only Janáček sat with the audience in the stalls of the theatre. After the great success of his work, he took a bow from his place in the audience. His beautiful and expressive grey head attracted and surprised the listeners. From the work they heard they had expected to see a revolutionary youngster. The great success spilled over into the street, where Janáček leaving the theatre, was applauded and cheered by enthusiastic Dutch, English and German admirers.

These are the stories told us by Janáček's loyal colleagues, our teachers. I shall follow them by some of my personal recollections of him.

He was born in Moravia in 1854 and christened Leoš. The name was well-chosen, for throughout his life he proved himself lion-hearted, as I shall hope to show. He possessed, however, another quality which I feel lay even deeper than his courage, and which he was always trying to express through his inborn musicality. I am speaking of the sense of wonder with which we are all born, but which most of us throw aside so easily and so early in our lives. Throughout his life he felt wonder and enjoyment in the life around him — in nature, in animals, in flowers and birds, and above all in the every-day life of the people around him. Janáček could echo the Psalmist, ''The heavens declare the glory of God and the firmament sheweth His handiwork''.

These qualities filtered through to me as a student under his direction. Very shy and self-conscious I felt as I walked up the pleasant tree-lined Smetana Street to become a student at Brno Conservatoire. It was the month of September 1927 and I was one of the youngest students — only seventeen and a bit. By now there were 200 students, all of whom felt grateful and proud as well as shy, as they passed Janáček's little house within the grounds of the conservatoire. We all knew that we owed our chance of becoming musicians to the courage and perseverance of one man. I also knew that I was fortunate enough to be joining an establishment with avant garde ideas on the teaching of music, but just what the new outlook was I had no very clear idea.

I did, however, know what Janáček had achieved in practical terms. In 1882 he had founded an organ school with nine pupils and three teachers. When the new Republic of Czechoslovakia was established in 1918, the school was ready to become a State Conservatoire with 186 pupils, 13 teachers and its own buildings.

My first impression of him confirmed my feelings of nervousness and shyness, although he, himself, would have laughed at the idea that he was frightening. He was a stocky, rather tubby figure, full of energy, surmounted by an abnormally large head of bristling silver hair and blazing blue eyes which lent force to all he said.

His speech was very characteristic, and most alarming. His words came out in staccato patterns like a cross between a machine gun and a typewriter. All his life he spoke with a Lachian accent. He often gave his operatic characters speech rhythms typical of his own way of talking, as in *Katya Kabanová*, where the matriarch says, ''You must learn bet-

ter manners...better manners...better..manners''. If one of
his pupils showed a lack of originality in composition, a
favourite rebuke was to rap out, ''What's in your head,
boy? Straw?''

With the exception of a year in Leipzig and Vienna for
musical education, Janáček spent his whole life in Brno.
When I knew him, his new ideas had already gained acceptance in the musical world around him, and he was becoming a world name in music. In his sixties and during the last
ten years of his life, he wrote *Katya Kabanová*, *The Cunning Little Vixen* and *The Macropulos Affair*, all of which
gained an immediate success. Perhaps he summarised his
life in his triumphant second String Quartet, which expresses his failures and also the ultimate break-through to
happiness. Before this there were many bitter years, when
after the production of his great opera, *Jenufa*, in 1904, it
lay unacknowledged for nearly twenty years, and recognition, when it did come, was from Vienna and Germany
rather than from Prague.

We have already spoken of his great interest in the world
of nature. In the last year of his life, in the spring of 1928, I
saw him often sitting in his garden. He loved flowers as he
loved animals. Cowslips, snowdrops, violets gave him great
pleasure, and birdsong was his special delight. He had trained two hens to jump on the garden table to say 'goodnight'
to him before they went to roost. His two dogs, Čipera
(Lively One) and Čert (Devil), were constantly with him. He
made notes of their speech patterns, even including the
change of intonation in Čipera's voice when he changed
from a puppy to a dog. I cannot help feeling that as he sat
there in the sunshine, he was compensating himself with
these simple things for the dark thoughts of his last opera,
*The House of the Dead*. Before he left the world, he wanted
to record the misery of man in chains, and his belief in
redemption through that spark of divinity in every

character, however depraved, which will eventually lead mankind to light and freedom. The score is headed "In every man there is a spark of God".

He was an acute observer of life, especially in the sphere of sound; his interest in speech rhythms and in human beings was the basis of his revolutionary ideas about opera. He listened to the sounds the human voice made in different situations, and instead of expressing emotion through unrelated melodic line, he tried to convey it through actual sounds which the human voice uttered in particular situations. This is his most original contribution to the form of opera; an idea which today has gained worldwide recognition among operatic composers.

He often told his students how he constantly listened to the speech of people going about their normal occupations, and noted their intonations. "I don't need to understand the words", he said, "I can tell by the tempo and modulation of speech how a man feels; if he lies, or if it is just a conventional conversation. I have been collecting these speech rhythms for over fifty years, and I have an immense dictionary. These are my windows into the soul of man, and when I need to find a dramatic expression I have recourse to my library".

At the age of eleven he became a pupil in an Augustinian monastery, where the boys were given general education and a specialised education in Church music so that they could participate in the services and celebrations of the monastery. It was here that he first developed his deep love of Moravia, and an enthusiasm for all things Slavonic, which was to colour his music throughout his life. Later he entered a Teachers' Training College and worked there for some years after his graduation. He also studied at the Organ School in Prague, and later in Leipzig and Vienna. He worked extremely hard and acquired a habit of strict discipline in work, which he passed on to his pupils. "First

you must know the rules'', he would tell us, ''then
sometimes you can afford to break them''. The early years
of his life were not happy, because while he worked
relentlessly at acquiring technical mastery, he was aware
within himself that he had something new to say in the
world of music, yet did not know as yet what it was — only
that he was dissatisfied with the prison in which conventional musical training fettered his creative spirit.

Perhaps the first happiness that Janáček achieved in
music was in his collections of Moravian folksongs, under-
taken in collaboration with František Bartoš, the famous
Czech philologist. He went first to Hukvaldy, his native
region, where he realised that much that he had to say in
music was based in the life of this part of the country. The
songs reflected the hard life his people led. His famous
_Lachian Dances_ are a fruit of this experience. From there he
went on to Southern Moravia where the songs and dances
were much more sparkling and gayer. Wherever he went he
made friends with local people, who therefore were ''not
shy to sing and dance in front of the gentleman from Brno''.

This is how he felt about folksong, ''I have lived in it
since childhood: in folksong the entire man is enshrined, his
body and soul, his milieu, everything. He who is rooted in
folksong becomes a complete man''.

Even in my day his interest in folksong was undiminish-
ed, although he was then over seventy. On Sundays he used
to walk with some of his students to Moravian festivals in
outlying villages, talking of music all the way. The exhausted students used to be glad to climb on a bus for the
journey home — not so Janáček, who looked forward to the
walk back.

He was a real father to his students and took a great interest in their progress and their circumstances. If someone
was absent he would sometimes call at his lodgings to see
what was the trouble. If the student was merely taking a day

off, this could be rather embarrassing.

The manner of his death was typical of his life — he died trying to help somebody. He was on holiday at Hukvaldy when a young girl went missing from the village, and he insisted on joining in the search. He became overheated and exhausted; complications set in, and he died in the hospital at Ostrava on August 12th 1928.

His death was a grievous shock to the world of music, but especially to Brno Conservatoire and the Opera House. The consolation for us, his students, was that he had formed on his teaching staff a band of colleagues who were deeply imbued with his principles. They were determined that his contribution to music should live on.

This was his credo:

"Grow out of your innermost selves

Never renounce your opinions

Do not toil for recognition

But always do all you can

So that the field allotted to you may prosper"

These principles he carried out unswervingly in his own life. He counted it a worthwhile task to put Brno and Moravia on the musical map of Europe, and in doing so he wrote his own name into the history of music.

In 1974, after an absence of over thirty years, I went back to the little house in the grounds of the old Brno Conservatoire (now the Janáček Museum). All was as formerly, even Pani Janáčková's mending basket was in its accustomed place. Over all brooded the spirit of the great Janáček,

"What's in your head, boy? — Straw?"

"I hope not, Mistře, I hope not".

# PREFACE

## by Margaret Tausky

Janáček was possibly the most acute listener in the sphere of music this world has ever known. He led, and indeed continues to lead, with the modern principle that music should be derived from the sounds that the composer hears around him. This, of course, had been unconsciously the case for many generations. How else would one account for Mendelssohn's *Fingals' Cave*, Rossini's *William Tell Overture*, Wagner's *Ring* and the awareness developed by the Impressionists?

But Janáček extended the use of these sounds to include those made by the human voice in its various moods. This new kind of listening naturally affected the material he used when it came to writing opera, and through the development of that gift he became a revolutionary in the field of music. His music is also full of the sounds made by the animal kingdom, with special regard to birdsong. In one of the most attractive operas, *The Cunning Little Vixen*, he mixed, most successfully, the sounds of nature, of animals and of human voices.

Not only did he hear the sounds around him with incredible accuracy, but even more wonderfully he trained himself to analyse these sounds into musical notation. This means that we hear in his music not only the tempo and rhythm produced by, let us say, a rainstorm, but our emotion is further aroused by the sound of the raindrops themselves, heard in the music.

Janáček however was not only a musician, he was a man of wide sympathies, and a great extrovert, who needed to express himself not only through music, but also through words. When he spoke at the opening of the Brno Conservatoire, which was established largely through his own efforts in 1920, he said:

> The gates of music are opening, and its tones are not restricted to the field of music. The laws of music exist in all living beings, in rhythm and in melody, and by these rhythms we measure ourselves and the universe......There could be nothing better in the mind of the whole nation than its motifs of words. At the Conservatoire we want to contribute to the riches of the Czech language.

And so it came about that he wrote regularly feuilletons and articles for the Brno daily paper, a national paper published in Brno, of rather the same standing as the old *Manchester Guardian*.

In these articles he wrote of all the everyday things that had commanded his attention in nature, in birdlife and in human situations. In reading of the thoughts of Janáček the man, we shall find much to illuminate our understanding of his music.

What he preached he practised and as a result we have these illuminating articles, which open to us both the man and the musician.

Where the subject-matter would be obscure for today's reader we have incorporated explanatory notes, and in some places notes on the geographical situations which he is describing. Sometimes the continual use of the word "little" may seem fulsome, but it must be understood that whenever one speaks tenderly or protectively of someone or something in Czech, it is usually natural to use a diminutive form.

It will be found that there is a common shape to many of the articles. They begin with a description of the subject, then his reflections and memories of it, often without regard to the time factor. In the middle of a thought or happening he remembers an occasion perhaps of thirty or forty years before, he comments, and then returns, without explanation, to the original subject. The article often ends with some philosophising or sometimes in a cheeky, humorous vein.

"And this is why I never forget to put in a solo for timpani."

In these pages Janáček opens his mind to you. May they help to deepen your love and understanding of the man and his music!

# INTRODUCTION

Hukvaldy, his native village.

Amid the hills of the Beskyd mountains, near Příbor, proudly there rises skyward a majestic castle, still well preserved. At its foot is the simple village school of Hukvaldy, and to the village schoolmaster was born, on the 3rd of July 1854, a son — Leoš Janáček.

The village of Hukvaldy was so dear to the great composer, that all through his life he was happy to return there, whenever he was free. There he could either rest in the fresh mountain air of the quiet Lachian village after his tiring teaching and creative work, or meditate on any new work he was planning. Many of Janáček's works were written in Hukvaldy. His last opera *The House of the Dead* underwent its final revision there, and his unfinished symphonic poem *Dunaj* (the Danube) was planned and sketched out in Hukvaldy.

In order to secure a quiet corner for refreshing himself and work, he bought a little house in Hukvaldy where he could think and create during his leisure hours. In his later years he, as a resident of Hukvaldy, increased his estate by purchasing a tract of forest land, where he loved to roam. As a faithful son of Hukvaldy, in his will he bequeathed his estate to the village.

Even in Brno he often thought of the quiet village in the Beskyd mountains which taught him the sweetness of the Lachian dialect, and the Lachian songs. In his literary sketches we often find reminiscences of Hukvaldy, of Šmolik the mayor, the forester Sládek, and other villagers whose company he enjoyed whenever he visited the village.

# MEMORIES OF YOUTH

## *My Lachia*

[All the rivers mentioned are Moravian, and tributaries of the Oder. This article shows how Janáček used to mix his scholarly friends from Brno; professor and poet Vladimír Šťastný, and Professor Batek, a language-teacher with local people, who kept alive the traditional music and dance.

He was seeing for the first time the Lachian dances, which were sung and danced by Sofie Harabiš, the daughter of a gamekeeper. The score of the *Lachian Dances* dates from this time. František Bartoš (1837 - 1906) was a Czech philologue.]

The river Lubina falls from the ridge of the Radhošt moun-tain over a precipice into an abyss.

The Ondřejnice flows through the village of Měrkovice, where it is so shallow that geese may bathe in it. The waters of the Oder in Košatec are still waters that run deep. The river Ostravice is the colour of steel, which is made in that region.

"Oh, rivers, which sing your way through Lachia, where are you hurrying?"

Under the Hukvaldy castle, in the little valley, looking so small that it could be overthrown by a stone, was the little inn "Harabiš", the windows of which shine through the dusk like fire. Inside you could cut the air, thick with smoke and the smell of humanity.

Sofie Harabišová flies from arm to arm. What a dancer! But that is a memory of forty-five years ago.

I am sitting bent over the proofs of the *Lachian Dances*.

In the notes, in the bars, I see the closely-packed room full of people, redfaced and sweating; it is like a kaleidoscope of moving, turning, bending bodies.

Where is the poet Štastný or Professor Batek or Mrs Marie Jangová now? Gone, all gone, those who took part on that wild summer night!

Why should this score of the *Lachian Dances* go out into the world now, so many years later?

The reason is the broad basis of folk art.

It seems to me that the little rivers of Lachia are chased by the rhythm of its dances, as in old days; and as it was, so it is.

Around ''Harabiš'', the little inn, the wind blows on these stormy nights, as in my *Dymák* (a Lachian dance), then as now.

Beautiful country, quiet people, and a dialect as soft as if you were cutting butter.

František Bartoš said:''If the Czech nation didn't already have a standard language, I would promote the Lachian to it!''

In memory of that warm summer night with the starry skies above, the bubbling of the Ondřejnice, which sounds like gentle love-chatter, in memory of you who were witnesses of that warm night, and now sleep for ever, ---

In praise of my native country, my Lachia, this score will go into the world. This score full of flashing little notes, full of teasing songs, sometimes chattering, sometimes thoughtful.

May it sow happiness and conjure up many a smile!

Hukvaldy, 22nd May 1928

# The Harabiš Inn

[The ascent of the Old Woman's Hill (580 m) was a favourite walk of Janáček].

The "Harabiš" Inn stands in a narrow valley, steep on both sides, in which there is just enough room for the Ondřejnice stream, the road beside it.

On the left side is the bottom of the Kaznic slope; on the right the foot of the Old Woman's Hill. On a little piece of flat land huddles the "Harabiš" Inn.

On the slope of the Old Woman's Hill stand two or three cottages; in the direction of Měrkovice is a mill.

Now in early September evening shadows were beginning to gather and to darken the sky.

In the litle windows of the Inn the alluring red lights were already twinkling. When black night fell the red glow looked like a fire under a cauldron.

In the room a press of maids, grooms, women with children in their arms. They all came from Měrkovice, Kozlovice, and the musicians from Kunčice.

Body to body, passionate dancing. The air was suffocating and full of fumes of sweat.

We stand at the door, watching the flashing movement, the faces sticky with sweat; screams, whooping, the sounding fury of the musicians. It was like a picture stuck on a limpid grey background. There was astonishment on the face of the poet Šťastný, while I eagerly followed the boiling pot of the Lachian dances.

We couldn't wait until the end. Already the pale moon was showing us the way to Hukvaldy.

The farmers came to fetch the maids and grooms.

That was a long time ago. That was in 1881.
The "Harabiš" Inn is no more.......

                                                    30.11.1924.


# *Without Drums...*


[This is an account of an incident of his childhood in 1861.]


Two neighbouring villages. One higher up on the green slope of the hill, the other on the vast plain. From the little windows of the village on the plain, one can see the village above. The clear little stream Ondrějnice still jumps and romps over the stones of the mountain village Hukvaldy, but later glides lazily between the gardens of Rychaltice.

In the 1860's two amicable schoolmasters lived there, one for each village. To the one on the hillside the good God gave many children, on the other He bestowed more worldly goods.

Music and bees were the only joys of the schoolmaster of Hukvaldy. When he was invited to the lower and richer parish he took his music with him. All we children often made the pilgrimage with Daddy. I, with a lovely descant, and my sister with her violin, we filled the gallery where the choir sat. My father loved best to lead his Sunday guests to the lower garden, where the bees were. The beehives stood there in a double row at an angle.

It was a beautiful Sunday. The schoolmaster from Rychaltice climbed up the hill to visit the schoolmaster of Hukvaldy. In the little summerhouse they chatted, and inspected the hives. The little windows of the hives were cleaned of cobwebs, so that one could see how the bees worked. We children were quite forgotten.

The licking of honey from plates and knives was soon finished.

Off we went to the farm belonging to the manor, where the barn had a sloping roof to the road. In a trice we climbed up the roof, smooth as glass, we slid from top to bottom. The corrugated zinc metal was so hot in the sun that you could hardly hold your hand on it.

It is strange that everything else escapes my memory. But I do remember the inspection of our Sunday-best trousers, which took place on the spot. Both rectors returned from the lower garden a little too soon.

Surely this could not have been the reason that the friendship between the two masters cooled? Surely not because I persuaded little Janoš from Rychaltice to go roof-sliding on a hot holiday afternoon? Why should I be aware of a coolness? I was only seven years old! It must have been the altered atmosphere which even at that age I could feel and understand.

No more singing and playing in the Rychaltice choir gallery on Sunday afternoons! All finished! And there they had so many open music stands, a gilded organ with a lot of registers on both sides of the manual, and in the back, right by the window two drums, as large as dough troughs; timpani!

Easter Sunday was approaching. In our school we used to lay the blackboard on the benches and sit around it. There we learnt the Mass, the special Mass for Hukvaldy! But was it worth it? There were violins, the holy trumpets, clarinets, but — it can't be done without drums, it isn't triumphant.

In the evening the shadows of ancient trees spread over the grass verges which reach right up to the church.

"Come on, don't be afraid! We are already by the churchyard."

Sh, sh! The gate is open, the church porch as well. Still a strong smell of incense from the High Mass. Up the creaking steps, oh, how terribly creaky, up to the choir gallery.----

Back we ran over the field, helter skelter --Timpani for Hukvaldy! It seemed as if the hills grew higher on purpose, and the sweat poured off us.

Again, I have forgotten. I don't know how we were greeted. Neither do I remember how the drums got back to the window of the Rychaltice gallery.

The Mass was not triumphant. It was without drums. Their sticks beat hard on my back.

I don't know if my pilgrimage reconciled our fathers.

Both are resting now, friends again I like to think, there near the choir.

*And this is why I never forget to write a solo for timpani!*
Brno, 16th April 1911.

# The lights of the Midnight Mass

[In a characteristically elliptical style this reverie touches on several aspects of Christmas and childhood, which Janáček had experienced.

1. The Christmases he had spent in the home of Sládek, the forester in Hukvaldy.

2. This leads to reminiscences of his own childhood.

3. The midnight chimes recall the procession of the Mass.

4. Finally he recalls the death of his two-year old son.]

In the backroom Mrs Sládeček is lighting little candle after little candle on the Christmas tree. What light there is in every corner! Even in the darkness of the two windows the gentle flames of the little candles are mirrored. Every passer-by will stop to see this galaxy of light. You can't see the little cottages, only in the deep darkness, their golden windows.

"Devil!" (his name) say I to the dog, "Stand quiet, don't move! Don't you hear they are singing 'Christ is born'?"

Devil growled with a motif like the screech of a rough rope being wound.

Chrr - - ee - -

The ugly sound cut into the holy singing of the children.

A quiet, gentle song woven like a spider's web by the voices of two children. But the barking of Devil's resistance could still be heard.

Inside the cottage a little girl kneels by the table, so small that the shadow of the corner falls across her face. Only her wide open eyes are in the light. The boy, who is also kneeling is taller, his head is level with the table top.

Then, suddenly jumping up, the dog growls again and

runs to the lime trees, and from there, his black footprints mark the snow in a circle, to the neighbouring cottage. In front of him something thin, like an exclamation mark, flashed by and disappeared in a gap near the shed.

In the room is unquiet.

Through the frozen windows, and in spite of Čert's barking you could hear the clatter of my carriage.

Mrs Sládečková, lamp in hand, peers out to look for the expected guest. So the Gentleman *did* arrive!

The children don't join in welcome, I call Čert, who runs in, winds himself between us, and frightens them with his name: "Čerte, Čerte" (Devil!) How can one finish the carol? Lidka has already peeped at her Christmas bonnet, and the boy eagerly shows me his rabbit hutch.

What a happy Christmas! And on St. Nicholas' day, and at Three Kings (Epiphany) a real devil appeared in the village. Wherever he turned up the children ran away and hid behind the fence. They thought about him for some time after however!

Healthy and happy we lived to another Christmas. The boy began to go to school — but he didn't get on very well.

A country child who feels with every little bird that chirps, who guesses where the bee flies from the hive, who is aware of even the little stones at the bottom of the clear stream, why do your eyes flit over the page, as if they were full of obstructions?

"First the Roman Empire was ruled by Kings — Tarquinius — cruelties — man-hood; but the kow is so fin, shee as not bin fed."

Why is it you remember now how your mother reproached you so long ago?

To lose your way from the Romans to a brown cow in the field!

These columns of verbs! Nineteen verbs in one column! Substantives from Aegyptus to Vergilius, adjectives from altus to septimus! Instead each little flower wanted to be named, every little insect on the path, the flying nightingale, the hungry fox and the fly on the window.

You had to answer questions until your head buzzed. What is this!...This?...and that?

But for you life lay in the world of nature.

And now? Rome, Athens — Přibor. Yes Přibor! — Gladly I shouted: Přibor! This had some meaning for me.

We were looking for Mamma returning from the fair by the river. Sometimes we went as far as Hill meadow before we met her. From Hill Meadow you can already see Přibor Tower. Four times it hides behind the hills before you reach the town. Once we went to the fair. People, shops, a great conglomeration of goods, crowds of people jammed together until you felt faint.

For half of the way home the legs still worked, but for the other half — mother's back, still nibbling the Přibor bun.

"Přibor", I call, and my heart is full. But what do I care about Athens or Rome?

Midnight strikes!

In the cold choir gallery they are singing the Midnight Mass.

The bars of the *Pastoral* by Sepf sleepily rock a lullaby, which floats above the misty spaces of the church.

"You are not singing, you rascal!"

These rough words to the student who carried the lanterns to the little church under the castle.

"So to forget yourself!"

The rebuke pulled him up just as he reached the processional cross!

"It was only for a little while" — (a happy little while.)

Mrs Sládek was again lighting little candle after little candle, but more than once she wiped away a tear with her pinafore. This year Lidka stopped after the first line of her carol:

Na·ro·dil se nám sy·ne·ček, po·sí·lá·me k vám.

Born to us a little boy whom we sent to you

She felt too sad to finish it.

The Gentleman didn't arrive either; he only sent a letter to say that the little son will never go to school.

Never before did the little candles go out so quickly on the Christmas tree.

Dark and quiet was the cottage when Sládeček returned from the forest. As he slung his gun into the corner of the room, it made a noise, as if to say:

"What the devil have we done to deserve this!"

Brno, 24th December 1909.

# My girl from the Tatra

[In 1875 Janáček spent a vacation in Vnorov with his uncle, a priest. Vitězslav Hálek was a great Czech poet, who wrote *The girl from the Tatra*. Later, this countryside of Moravia on the borders of Slovakia became the milieu for his opera *Jenufa.*]

The student fell in love with Betty Gazarek. A girl like a flower, from the farm at Vnorov.

He didn't tell her of his love and how could she guess something so stupid!

For him she became *The girl from the Tatra*.

For that reason he walked with a copy of Hálek's poems, as a priest might carry the Host.

This was his Tabernacle.

The end of the holidays came, and with it the end of a fairy tale.

"Anči, take this! Give this little book to Betty. Don't forget, straight away when you get back!"

Anči, the maid from the vicarage, carried the student's luggage on her back.

Then he walked sadly through the wonderful oak woods to the railway station of Písek. This wood is completely felled now. Even in those days it seemed to me that there were not enough of life's tribulations in that poem of Hálek's, it was all too smooth. And Betty was not really suitable for *The Girl from the Tatra*. I don't know......I have never read the poem since then.

In 1926 nobody in Vnorov remembered Betty Gazarek.

1.4.1927.

# My town — Brno

[In 1865 Janáček, aged 11, was accepted as a choirboy into the King's Cloister in Brno. He describes the Brno of 1866 at the time of the Prussian war.

He goes on to speak of his lessons with Nerudová, a famous violin virtuoso.

The final paragraphs blaze out his joy and triumph in the liberation of Czechoslovakia in 1918. He tells us this was the inspiration of his *Sinfonietta*.]

It was the year 1866.

From St. Anne's hospital in Baker Street to the monastery in King's Street there was a constant to-ing and fro-ing. Cholera raged, there were a lot of funerals and we little singers attended them.

Then the monastery square was full of Prussians, like swarms of black ants.

Only yesterday our own soldiers were there, but now they have vanished.

The millstream from the Monastery gate — Vincenc Brandl lived in the adjoining house — flowed, lazy and dirty, to run under the little bridge.

From Baker Street one went over the little bridge into Cross Street.

By the bridge was a cross.

Tracks passed each other frantically, and then in the sudden curve a car skidded and turned over. Sacks flew out, and from the torn sacks poured coffee. The narrow pass blocked! I witnessed all this.

Opposite St. Anne's cowered a small house. It had a solitary window on the first floor. On the ground floor one went down a few steps into our shoe-maker's shop.

Ach, he was an unbelievable grumbler!

"Repair this? Heels gone, uppers like wings, there is nothing to hold them together!"

Behind the hospital lay the school called Lakerwiese, and behind that the smelly tanning factory.

Thus far we were familiar with the town, but further on we should have been lost.

As a bigger boy I usually went to my violin and piano lessons past the Hutter pond.

A pond? It was really a swamp and a rubbish dump and a long alley of chestnuts. Behind that, in a lonely house there lived the virtuoso Vilhelmina Norman-Nerudová, my teacher.

As for the Lužánky Park my days were so full, that for me it might as well never have existed.

And to the Black Fields? They spoke for the anguish of the workers.

In those days Brno was a small town.

On the outskirts were the town cemetery and the St. Wenceslas Cemetery, called the Old Cemetery, the church of Zabrdovice and the hospital run by the Sisters of Charity.

The Elizabeth Convent was in those days an isolated building.

To go to the Pisárky Park and the Yellow Hill was practically an expedition.

One could really explore the whole town on foot.

You could walk from the long bridge over the Svratka river to the Viennese bridge through the court of the Ypsilanti house, on whose gate, carved in stone, was a Turk sitting crosslegged, along the tannery to the Serpent fountain, under the František church. From there into the dark, gloomy cellarlike room, No. 7 Old Brno street along which I hurried every day when I taught at the Organ School.

Run, it is all right to run! But how could one be in love with the Brno of those days?

One day suddenly I saw a miraculous change in the town.

My antagonism to the gloomy town hall vanished, my hatred of the Špilberg jail, inside whose depths so much misery had been suffered, disappeared, and with it my antipathy to the street and those who swarmed there.

Over the town the light of freedom blazed, the rebirth of Oct, 28th 1918!

I was part of it, I belonged to it.

The blare of victorious trumpets, the holy quiet of the King's Convent, night shadows and the gentle breeze from Green Hill.

The beginning of upsurge and greatness in our town gave birth to my *Sinfonietta* which carries this understanding of my town — Brno.

24.12.1927.

"...... and back to Hukvaldy again. I'm building on to my house and getting it ready for my old age."

Janáček's study. ''...... I always get new ideas there.''

# THE SOUNDS OF MUSIC

## *Introductory words on the opening of the Conservatoire in Brno*

[Here we learn of the hopes aroused in the heart of Janáček himself by the formation of the new Conservatoire. In the first year of the new State Constitution the Brno Conservatoire was opened in 1919 with Janáček as the first principal. These are his words on that very important occasion.]

I have written about you before, robins! Modest little birds, lovable and trusting, round little bodies, which one would like to caress. You sing the same tune whether in the bosky Lužánky Park in Brno, or in the old acacia trees of the Prague embankment.

Just as it is certain that our own life makes us smile or sigh, so that the light or shadow of our mood shows in our tone, so it is certain that in the case of the robin neither the flowers of the Lužánky Park, nor the silvery shine of the Vltava have any influence on his song. He is a very limited little fellow.

In the season of love he sings of desire in these three motifs: in three-and-a-half seconds!

*Note:* The music above is in Janacek's own hand and its engraved version alongside. In the following pages Janacek's original notation will only be used when it is easily legible.

He finishes his melody, and then repeats it, exactly as before with the same eagerness.

I was listening once when my robin broke off the flow of the motif. A blackbird flew clumsily by, almost hitting him. I thought the robin would continue and finish his song. But no, he began again — the first motif, the second, the third.

The season of love is over. Through the fallen leaves, now covered with snow, he hops about uttering only a single note.

Who would like to teach a robin to sing?

Who would like to teach somebody to be a composer?

He who composes was born to it. One can't be taught to compose music.

You yourself create your composition. Keep your inspiration secret, and your work upon it. Don't hamper clarity of execution with dependence on other people's style, and don't stifle it with outside influences.

Only an experimental field is the source of true learning.

Everything must be scientifically prepared, then narrowed and separated. Thus will you get grain without chaff. From the grain the seed germinates in your creative mind. You may build yourself a Temple of Creation, and lose yourself in it, but still discipline your inspiration, so that it doesn't become diffused. By experimental musical psychology you will reap a richer harvest.

I heard the robins sing in 1914.

This year, in the upheaval of our liberation, they sing the same song, and they always will, their young, and their young's young, for as long as they are charmed by love's desire.

This is the truth about expression.

Can we find it as easily in man?

Why do I call for robins, robins for the Conservatoire?

For the method of scientific work.

A simpler love song than that of the robin is the tone with which a bee flies from the hive.

On this single note it flies into the distance, it seems haphazardly. They say a bee doesn't recognise the flowers as separate units, but in some way they do recognise the shape and colour of them.

And how does it fly back to the right hive at the end of that journey which we cannot follow?

The sustained tone, constant and unvarying suggests to us an eager search, a sharp mind, and a consciousness full of impressions lived through and remembered.

Shall I recruit even you, my little bee, into the Conservatoire? Didn't Charpentier learn from you the effect of a single tone in *Louise?*

And so we enter upon a new life of the Conservatoire of music.

The gates of music are opening and its tones are not restricted to the field of instruments. The laws of music exist in all living beings, in rhythm and in melody and by these rhythms we measure ourselves and the universe.

There is nothing better in the robin's mind than its song. There could be nothing better in the mind of the whole nation than its motifs of words. At the Conservatoire we want to contribute to the riches of the living Czech language.

A pair of robins! Happily they hop about my garden. How lovely now in the autumn are their gentle voices!

(ui -- u - ti!)

Why do I always return to them?

I want such composers, robins, who compose out of the very necessity of their being, who can fill the skies with explosions of sound, but also those who know the value of — silence.

Brno, 30th September 1919.

## The Beginning of a Novel

[The title of this article was also the title of one of Janáček's first national operas.

The Hipp's Chronoscope, to which he refers, was a clockwork instrument for measuring very small intervals of time, which was shown as on a clock's face.]

It was on the evening of the 15th February 1922. Twilight at six o'clock by the railway station.

On the pavement the taller one, with rosy cheeks in a red overcoat flounced petulantly.

She said scornfully:

We'll stand here but I know he won't come

Her friend, paler in a shabby dark jacket, followed the last
note with a sad echo:

What does it matter?

She didn't move, half through obstinacy, half still
expectant.

I went away, carrying this short conversation in my mind
— later I put it down in music.

From a distance I turned round; in the mist the two
friends became one wavering dark shadow on the white
snow.

My guess is that each of their life stories will go a different
way.

I shall now enrich the tonal beauty of the conversation:

Dear little girls, you were quite unaware of the tonal
beauty of your conversation. You couldn't guess that with
it you revealed your feelings and much more!

Everything about the method of composition has been already discovered except the mystery of the source of our inspiration.

These mysteries can be uncovered in the tones the music takes, at first unconsciously, but later the tones will be found to have originated in speech.

Now I am going to measure accurately the length of the whole conversation.

This I am able to do by the aid of Hipp's Chronoscope given me by Dr. Vladimir Novák. The count by my own method coincides with the count on the HCh.

The whole conversation lasted ·4029 of a minute.

It is not difficult in this way to measure the length of a quaver in twenty conversations. I add to the tone the vibration between syllables for those must be counted too.

We are now on the path that leads to the source of inspiration.

If there were no tones, surrounded by different vibrations, many times used in speech, (although unconsciously) no musician could use them in his compositions.

What about the sad one of the two friends?

"What does it matter?" Did she wait there, whether he came or not?

Madam Butterfly?

Did she wait in vain?

Brno, 17th March 1922.

# Glagolitic Mass

[This mass was written at the instigation of the Archbishop of Olomouc, Leopold Prečan, to whom the work is dedicated. It was written in Luhačovice between the 2nd August and 15th October 1927. The first performance was on 5th December 1927.]

Why did I write it?

It rains, it pours in Luhačovice. From the window I look up at the frowning face of the Komona mountain.

The clouds pile up; the storm tears them apart, breaks them up.

Exactly as when a month ago we stood in front of the school at Hukvaldy in the rain.

And next to me stood the archbishop.

It is getting darker and darker. Now we are looking into the black night; zigzags of lightning cut the sky open.

I light the wavering electric light bulb high on the ceiling.

I sketch just the quiet motif of the desperate cry from the soul: "God have mercy".

Then only the joyous shout "Glory, Glory!"

After that the tearing sorrow in the motif: ''He suffered,
was tortured and buried.''

Then the credo and the unconquerable faith in the motif:
''I believe''.

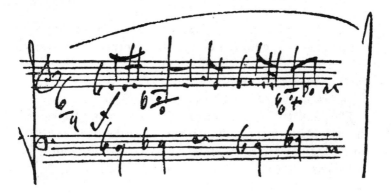

And the release of emotional turmoil in the motifs:
''Amen, amen!''

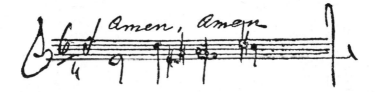

The holy reverence in the motifs of the ''Sanctus'', the ''Gloria'' and the ''Agnus Dei!''

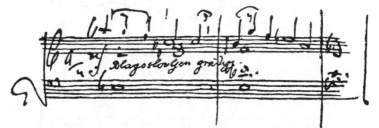

In motifs without the darkness of the catacombs of the Middle Ages.

Without the usual lines of imitation,
without the pathos of Beethoven,
without the playfulness of Haydn;
contrary to the paper technique of Witt, which estranged our Křižkovský!

Tonight the crescent moon shines on little pieces of paper full of notes — tomorow the sun will seek them in curiosity.

At first my fingers were frozen — then through the open window the warm air streamed in, laden with the scent of the moist forests of Luhačovice — this was my incense.

The cathedral became for me the enormous grandeur of the mountains, beyond which stretched the open sky into misty distances; in those distances a flock of sheep rang the little bells.


I hear in the tenor solo, the celebrant,
in the soprano, a girl, — an angel,
in the choir, the Czech people.

The candles are high fir trees in the forest, lit by stars; in the ritual somewhere in the misty distance I see a vision of St. Wenceslas.

In the language I hear the missionaries, Cyril and Method.

Before three weeks of evenings in the Spa of Luhačovice had passed, the little work was finished; mainly so that Dr. Nejedlý shall have some justification for saying I compose like a Berlitz crash course — easily and quickly!

On 5th December in the Stadium in Brno the *Glagolitic Mass* will be performed. I praise in advance the singing of Mr Tauber and Mrs Cvanová. Also the few notes — but healthy ones — of Miss Hloušková and Mr Němeček. I praise the fresh voices and the secure intonation of the chorus.

Even Mascagni was satisifed with the orchestra and I am sure that the Brno Philharmonic Society will be satisfied with the conductor, Jaroslav Kvapil.

Brno, 23rd November 1927.

# Why do we have so many waltzes and polkas?

Every dance has its choreographic theme, which is supported by a musical theme. The turning in a circle to four or three in a bar is the smallest and simplest theme. Even children can dance to a polka or waltz. But we can dance to any kind of music. The simpler the dance the more will music of this character be written.

Among these writers we find the names of many famous composers.

In the complicated choreogaphic themes of Moravian folk dances it it quite different. We remember the rather complicated steps by a definite tune. The people perform the steps of Pilky and Čeladenský (two of the Lachian dances) when they hear the tune they know so well. The musicians are allowed to make only slight variations on this tune.

It is this style of folk dance which must be preserved. Only a professional ballet company could dance Pilky and Čeladenský to new music of this, or any other, composer. These dancers can also perform to the beat of a stick on the floor.

In Moravia we have about 300 dances, and so neither the waltz or the polka were really our folk dances. Their simple choreographic themes were only one component among other richer themes.

Today it is quite different, even among the folk dancers; they perform only two dances, polka and waltz, and the music to them....

a shame!

a scandal!

9.7.1905.

# From Professor Torraca's lecture

[Professor Torracca (1853-1938) was an Italian historian and literary critic who gave a lecture on Dante, which Janáček attended.]

## When I heard his words

And later in the course of his impassioned speech, full of pathos:

Can't you imagine how these words would sound in the immortal poet's own mouth? I heard the name "Beatrice" melting in the fire of love.

8.6.1921.

# Smetana's daughter

She was in the shop buying a lemon. I hear her greeting.

Good-day

So I waited outside the shop for her. On the way to Smetana House she asked me:

How long are you staying?

I wrote down her speech.
She:

Music?

I explain to her that with what she inherited from her father perhaps she inherited the way he spoke.
She:

That interests me very much

--he would say, if he saw his speech written in music motifs.

I am sixty-three years old

she says, when I admire the low register of her voice.
But in singing she is a soprano, she says.
I speak to her of her father's house in Litomyšl.
She:

I don't think it is very nice

I ask her if she wouldn't like to live there in the winter, and in Luhačovice in the summer.
She would like to do that.
I say "Perhaps Litomyšl will offer you the chance."
She is surprised how quickly I write the notes in music.
She:

Can you pitch an 'A'?

Her father could.
She:

I can only sometimes

I say: "You speak very quietly."
She:

Quietly?

I was surprised, because people say she is so highly strung.

She asks me when I compose. I answer, "In the mornings."

She:

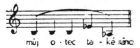

My father too wrote in the morning

When she agrees in conversation, it always comes with a typical half-question:

Don't you think?

Have you heard how a little child imitates a kitten?

Me-ow

What about a grumbling old woman?

What about the student of a strict professor? He emphasises every syllable and with each emphasised accent his voice rises as if he were climbing a ladder?

Then you must remember there is a contortion of the mouth of the speaker.

When we repeat in a conversation somebody else's words we are already practically in the theatre.

For we repeat them as if the person we know were actually present.

Then we must consider the speed of speech, the gentle or rough voice, a singing tone, nasal breathing, a mumbling voice. There is also an angry expression, a reproachful look, the wish to flatter. Again there is the tone register of the speech and sometimes a sing-song fall.

In re-creating these it is as if we bring the person we know to life, whether far away or near, whether alive or in eternity!

There are plenty of living examples — and I have many, many proofs.


Smetana's daughter went on to tell me that her father looking at the score of *Hubička* (The Kiss) said:

All this will be valued one day

In saying this, in citing Smetana's own words, I could hear he himself speaking. Thus, I guess, spoke Bedřich Smetana.

Here, probably emotionally excited, in the hope of the future success of his work.

A very short fragment of the Master's speech through the truth of a passing idea reaches us through his daughter.

Of course the register of the Master's speech would be an octave lower; it would lie in the higher part of the Great Octave. The rhythm of equal stresses and the melodic fall would be the same.

I am glad of this example.

Now the conversation became painful.

I say: "I hope they remembered you at your father's celebrations. Please tell me honestly, did they remember you with a financial present?"

She (quietly):

Chraň pan - bu!"

God forbid!

Formerly she used to get 300 crowns from the National Theatre in Prague, now she gets — 4000.

I am sitting in her little room in Luhačovice. Surely it can't be Smetana's daughter to whom I am saying: "Who was it who attacked you so rudely by Jansky's clinic, near the post office, so roughly that people stopped...."

She; "The Bailiff.....he commandeered the divan you are sitting on, and..."

I jumped up from the commandeered divan as if I had been bitten.

Unfortunately this kind of thing happens quite often nowadays.

Brno, 3rd December 1924.

# Wells and fountains

[This article shows how familiar Janáček was with the waterways around his native village of Hukvaldy, which he explored on his lonely walks.

He dedicated this article to Alois Král, who discovered the caves of Demänov and made them accessible to the general public. He had been at one time a pupil of Janáček.]

Their surfaces are limpid. Their waters never dry up nor freeze. They mirror the flight of a butterfly, and the dark shadows of the dense forest, which stare into them with the unwavering gaze of a child.

A fallen leaf sinks to the bottom contentedly, so it seems to me. Before she drinks, the tiny wren chases away the sadness of solitude with a little song.

The hind drinks from them with a gentle kiss.

*The wells of Hukvaldy.*

I know *The Fox's Well.* A slender beech bestrides it, but it cannot arrest the gush of flowing water. The little waves dance over the white stones, and run headlong into the Fish stream. A fox's family have made their den in a labyrinth of boulders, and it is there that they are hurrying.

*The Public Fountain.*

''A fine of ten crowns on those who fail to replace the cover.''

Of course for the fountain, when the cover is replaced, it is as if she closed her eyes.

Bucket after bucket, clean and unclean, is lowered and filled. At the outflow geese are cackling, in the puddles ducklings are splashing.

It is a pity that the fountain should be ill-used by the public. The sanitary police ought to see to it. The sun does not warm it, the little stars don't fall into it. Its waters are used for hogwash and chaff for the cattle.

A woman carrying buckets on a yoke says that the fountain is a public one on the village green in the shade of the blue-green plumtrees.

public one, a public fountain.

*The fountain beneath the castle walls* is handsome and inclined to show off in a gentlemanly fashion.

This is not so, this is not so

Through pipes the water runs the length of the manor farm, into the clerk's houses, into the watering places in the yards. It wets the malt in the brewery, boils the beer, and in distant pubs of the district reddens the faces, and leads to a lot of rubbishy talk.

Near the slaughter-house the water is coloured with blood. If you go through the tall grass in the overgrown avenue of melancholy old lime trees to the foot of the Kaznic hill there dreams the encased brickwalled Fish Fountain, now fallen into disuse.

Here stand three lime trees, and in their roots there hides a little well —

Yes, Helisov's

The little girl told me with a smile.

Longlegged spiders run about on its surface. As a little chap, I wondered how they are able to walk on the water.

In the left-hand corner the rippling spring shifts the clean sand. The green moss is caught at the bottom.

Two or three steps higher up flows the mill's ditch, muddied by constant rain, but the well is proud of its clear water, and the Babi mountain guards this little treasure.

What about that fountain?

By the Kolos?

asks Sladeček, the forester. They deepened it, lined it with stone, and at the bottom, except for the little spring, encased it with cement. What a horrible idea! A lot of worms fell in from the garden, and as they drowned they turned white.

From a distance of ten paces I hear it mumble and beat on the stone trough with a definite chord, but a confused rhythm:

Nearer to, it changes character.

Now I am above it, and hear with how much stronger a
voice it speaks to me!

I would like to look in,

The holy

fountain for a hidden water nymph. But by the voice I hear
it sounds more like a surly forester.

*The White Fountain* dreams of ancient times. They say that its source is in the springs of the deep well of Hukvaldy castle.

How gladly would this fountain sing pious Hussite songs, as well as the warlike ballads of Čapek of San and Hukvaldy! But---it is choked with the mud of fallen and decayed leaves.

Myths arise about fountains, and the deeds which take place around them. They live on in folksong. I remember:

"She was standing by the fountain
coaxing the peacock to drink.
Tell me, my darling,
if you love me?"

What rhythm there is in this amplification! Where else could such a simple situation be immortalised?

The silver surface of wells is motionless, but you look into the depths, and there at the bottom the spring boils with a ruthless seething.

What colours the blossoms throw on to the mirrored surface of the well! Sometimes a lively face, or a heavenly blue sky, sometimes it blushes with cold, pales with the dying sun, becomes green with the spring, yellow with the autumn. The silver of the stars is reflected in its depth.

Even the movements of the water are wonderful. How they chase each other when the storm breaks the naked black branches, or when the warm spring breeze bends the blossoms.

Even the stupid Janek from the Blodek opera *In The Well* knows about these faces.

A fountain is so beautiful, it is surprising that it wants to venture into the world.

Now the water hurries away, and in its hurry stumbles over every little stone. It chatters and shouts and grumbles: "Out of my way....out of my way!" it cries.

It is no more that quiet, languid, little fountain; the world has changed it so much.

I know a large fountain — nearly a small lake, choked by the darkness of ages.

When the curtains of eternal night were lifted through the skill and hard work of Alois Král what a miracle was there!

Within this eternal darkness grew a work of beauty tinged with a pink blush. On one side was a hem of delicate lace, broadly woven. Opposite hung clusters like ripening grapes.

There are no angels in this eternal darkness, only souls who play with countless marbles of pink and white. Into the little holes the stream wriggled and turned them. Surely they must have thrown them about as well — because there are a lot of them on the little lake.

There is a distant drone of menacing waters:

much more menacing nearby:

It fills the air. It is a warning. Nature puts forth this great miracle of the universe from under the earth's crust, in the caves of Demänov.

Nature arranges guards in every corner of the underworld — tall and perpendicular, midgets and giants, stalagmites and stalactites. Nature has given them vestments of white, pink, bloodred, and hung a black tapestry behind them.

Whether the water is quiet or surging Nature listens to it. She created monstrous cringing gnomes. How strange it must seem to these guards, when I wake them with their own speech, their own music!

They shake with joy at their awakening.

Sharp ears hear:

The chord of stalagmites covered with hoarfrost:

The groan of a falling fragment:

A play on strings woven from the living drops of water that are falling:

How gladly would I make it into a melody, eternal, awe-inspiring. It is woven of dense darkness, mixed with the roar of underground waters, surface streams crashing down into the chasm, screaming from the broad streams, wailing from the cliffs, and finally falling into the abyss.

Put out the lights!

Through the black darkness little invisible hammers ring out in the glorious workshop of Nature.

A drop of water has fallen:

Somewhere else the drops sing rhythmically:

They also ring, like bells:

And now quickly they tell of another world, before they are swallowed by the waves:

And here they rustle angrily:

When darkness comes the pink fountain of Demänov fades into the melancholy distance.

Without the whisper of these songs how sad it would be here, so near eternity.

Let there be light!

How much happier are you, you fountains, who can see the sun!

8.9.1922

# *Silence*

[In this short essay Janáček explains, in as detailed a manner as he is able, the birth of musical inspiration as he experiences it.]

When you look into the shallows of Ondrejnice in the Hukvaldy district you see — only water. Nothing is alive there — no fishes, no frogs. The sun is high in the sky, but the atmosphere is void — no glittering moth, no buzzing of a bumble-bee, no blue dragonflies measuring the stream from edge to edge with their big eyes, in readiness for their flashing flights.

A thrush comes every day right up to the house, tame and companionable, it hops behind the poultry.

In the fields the ears of corn, swollen by the frequent rain, sway drunkenly.

The green grass grows wild, as if it would never ripen and go to seed.

This year's summer! Quiet, silent. Even one's thoughts become silent too, longer and longer silences between them — and suddenly one hears a ringing in the ears. A gentle tremolo of different tones. I am choosing only the main tone;

But joined to it is a higher and a lower octave building into a chord.

These are the sounds which lead to an idea. What a mysterious path it is! The blood quickens, and it is only you who can hear the delicate echoes.

For me this is the music of life, this is the place, the moment when sounds shape themselves into an intellectual concept.

I hear the music constantly in the empty silence, while the intellect is still and all emotional strings are relaxed.

Have you too heard the ringing of this strange music? It comes from a central inner impulse when all around us is still as the grave.

Is it a response of the blood which is brought about through the activity of our thoughts?

It is not the same sound as when we say, ''somebody is thinking of me. In which of my ears did it ring?''

Or: ''You guessed it! Yes, they *are* thinking of me''.

It is not the painful tone which Smetana heard continuously ringing in his ear. It is the sound of silence, of creative inaction, laziness, tiredness, a pensive mood. It is a pedal tone, which can only be dispelled by an upsurge of creation.

A field of clover with a low fence to protect it from hens and geese. But what is such a fence for a little goat? With one leap she was in the clover. Alarmed, the shepherdess chased after her. She caught the little goat by all four legs, and carried her out of the field. ''You might get blown!'' she says to the little goat, who had hardly got to her feet when she was back in the clover again. Once more the shepherdess rescued her.

Then the little goat turned her head towards the shepherdess' face and licked her, after which she got to her feet and butted her little horns against her. A funny little scene!

I had a strange thought. Why has the little goat defended herself so soundlessly? She has such a clear nasal ''m'', and so beautifully articulated an ''e''. A human being could not emit a better bleat. Why does she not voice her defiance?

One can describe as fully as one may the articulation of our vowel sounds; there are not enough vowels in phonetic language to allow imitation.

The impulse to articulate lasts perhaps one hundredth of a second. But it is not enough to watch the movements of the mouth. The impulse is instinctive, but the emission of sound is combined with emotional texture and is often as light as gossamer.

You have surely noticed in humans an involuntary expression where there are feelings of horror, happiness, tears or laughter. Here you can observe a connection between articulation, postures, gestures and facial expression.

Why else should the little goat say only ''Me-e-e-e''?

When she has a tongue, a dainty mobile little tongue, which could say *rrrr* or *llll*! It is her lack of emotional development which limits her to utter only her *meee* on one tone.

What impertinence! A few musicians accompanied by some ragamuffins march in goose-step through the road beneath the castle, with twanging, beribboned instruments on their backs and singing as they go. A straggle of children come running to see the fun.

"Play for us!" they beg with giggles.

Just imagine that from the road beneath the castle walls they progressed to the castle grounds, and from there they turned back and actually sang a serenade in front of the kitchen of the nobility.

There are no police or guards to subdue such holiday-makers. Let us always put children first, and allow them to call: "Play for us"! They will soon enough vanish from the scene!

Through the deep forest of stately beeches I climb to the flat plateau which forms the courtyard of the old Hukvaldy castle. There stand centuries-old limes with their faded blossoms. There is quiet, not even a bee to be heard. High up in the limpid sky flies a swallow. A small dark bird with a little dark beak bounces comically up and down at intervals, and sits down near me on a stone. The forester's geese waddle lazily home, munching the ears of the tall grass as they go.

My eyes wander over the distant country. The mist mixes with the smoke of the factories of Vitkovice. One can hardly see the tower of Brušperk. Some of Přibor's roofs glisten in the sunshine, peering with curiosity at the countryside. The gloomy village of Kaznicov looks as if it were painted in dark colours. All is quiet. I think of the conservatoire in Brno. In a month the school year begins, yet here is such silence.

Again the tone of silence, inactivity, laziness, emptiness?
Perhaps tiredness?
I sit here lost in my dreams.

Hukvaldy, 15th August 1919

"The silver surface of the wells is motionless. You look into their depths and see the restlessly bubbling spring."

# BIRDS

## Spring

[Again and again in these pages Janáček shows his great sympathy and understanding of the world of nature, the animal kingdom, and his reverence for the mysteries of growth and renewal. But perhaps he feels closest kinship of all with the birds, for they, like he, are God's musicians.]

The little black eye looks up at me friendly, fearlessly; the little head is dark blue; the little back, crop and belly brown. The wings are striped in black and white. What little bird is this? Lužánky Park is full of its call.

Di - di - di - di - di - di   di

Again and again! How his little throat trembles with it! And now he has flown a little distance and laments:

Tio,   tio,   tio !

He dares to come right near me; pecks at something on the ground, hops a little and pecks again:

It is as if he commented every time: "It's very hard!"

Suddenly somewhere in the tree sounds a short-tempered motif, and the little bird at my feet answers in exactly the same tone as if he said: "Don't be afraid! Nothing is going to happen." And a company of blue mischief-makers took over the whole park.

The hillside looks as if it might turn into a cone. I am looking for a blackbird which made the hill ring with song. As if at a signal he settled on an acacia tree: black, ungainly, but with a golden song in his little beak. He looked into the distance, but I kept my eyes on him.

His first motif

comes from somewhere in the distance. He repeats it exactly. He seems to know for whom he is singing. He starts a new song:

Rather a sad one. With his little foot he scratched his little throat, and started again, more happily this time:

To - y - o  to  toyo to!

At intervals, quite measured ones, he sings just to himself:

Foo - ty !          Fo  tyo  tio!          Fo - ty - to  fo - ty - to !

The Coda of the song was definite; he screeched sharply

as he always does when he is scared. As every blackbird does — today, yesterday and forever more. He flew down and fell heavily into the bushes.

How many times does a cuckoo call his mate?

Ku - ku !

He never starts a trifle lower; on the contrary. His companion answers in the same way. And now they pursue each other in longing. Their songs become more and more urgent, rising higher, ever higher. Into the distant forest sank the last sound of the third with the notes *d* and *b flat*.

Ku - ku!

And man?

The high tides of Spring brought a lot of brushwood to the river banks. A poor old woman from Hranice explores the river Bečva with her skirt tucked up.

She peers into the dirty grass and from time to time her eyes scan the shining waves. Here she gathers a small stick, there a battered, washed-up root. Her bundle of firewood is slowly growing. She talks to herself quietly but intelligibly:

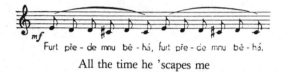

Furt pře - de mnu bě - há, furt pře - ce mnu bě - há.

All the time he 'scapes me

I think she is talking about a companionable fish.

This is the highest degree of absorption, talking to your own lost ego. A tightened string of the soul, which can only sound when you release it. Here along the bank poverty walked with dumbness.

There is no necessity for this diseased degree of tension, reaching a repetitious hardened expression. Bitter longing, wonder which confuses, big-eyed fear, the happy-go-lucky outlook of childhood, stinging spitefulness, hasty stumbling leading to a stutter: all these strung-up moods are like the boiling of bubbles, all displaying the same colour.

These sounds, so tenacious of their cause or reason, that when you lift the lid, uncover them, as in a draught, they vibrate with either the joy or grief of your soul. They are a recognisable password with which one can easily become the guest of someone else's soul. The little soul of a bird, the human soul of a man, it's all the same. They intrude violently for they are outcries of the soul! And the Spring has its password: everything rejoices, grows and lives!

14.6.1912

# These lovers
## (a Spring study)

The lawn is already dewy in the sunrise. The shadows of the trees glitter on it in the frost.

The blackbirds have finished singing their nocturne. Their legs are not freezing as they continually hop through the grass.

The constant song of the finches echoed through Lužánky Park and resounded from all sides. It seems as though their songs hung on every bush, hooked on with the first three notes, twined around the little branches with a trill, they swing on the thread of a long interval in the morning air. Suddenly I hear a quick, cheeky song:

Want a drink, want a drink, want a drink?

I want to put words to it: "Want a drink?"

This would cover the articulation of the bird's three notes. I am looking for the singer in the crown of the tree. There sticks out into the clear sky a little black branch, and on it a bird smaller than a blackbird. Grey on his tummy with black stripes. He has hardly drawn breath when he repeats his song:

You want more, you want more?

In less than a second he finishes the song, he recollects, and sings another:

and another:

and again another:

Now dreamily, wistfully, with a thin vowel ''eee'':

I can only just keep pace with one new song after another.

He sang forty-four in two minutes! Then he flew down onto the grass. A greenish little back, a thin little beak, black, sparkling eyes. A thrush.

Why should I feel surprise? A multitude of different melodies — identical melodies repeated — melodies separated only by a pause — melodies always lasting for less than a second.

An apprentice from the nearby Brno factory ran across the grass and disappeared into the twisting paths and bushes. The long wail of the factory hooter is calling the workers. Now the other apprentice runs across calling:

Jendo! (Jenik)

From the distance I can still hear:

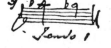

The rascal lengthens the call like a noose, in which he hopes to catch his companion. The call is prolonged in the effort to find each other.

And in this way our thrush calls too, but without any trace of emotion:

Quiet, quiet, quiet!

Well, somewhere here his consort is nesting! He knows how always to play on a different string. He has the songs in his little heart, as I said, forty-four of them! He easily varies them.

His singing is like a mosaic inscription, which reads ''Loving desire''. Each of the letters glitters with a different shimmer, and yet is quickly extinguished. The thrush's character is superficial. He has plenty of witty ideas, but he tears them up by their roots.

By the second song it appears as if he has already forgotten the first one. It seems to me as if he has no complicated reactions. Most of the time he is thinking of one particular melody and he usually ends his songtime with it. It is the melody: ''Want a drink, Want a drink?''

And his little consort, barely forty steps away, hardly hears his conversation, but continues to collect dried grass for a softer and warmer little nest.

But the thrush's little brain does quite remarkable work.

A human being speaks six syllables in a second, but the melodies of a thrush, though poorly articulated, are clearly tuned, and there are three or four in a second.

On 10th April 1922 at 7 in the morning all hell is let loose in Lužánky. The golden sun has lighted the whole park and all living things. The proud finches call right and left from all sides:

Já té mám moc     tu-ze!

I love you so much

(They over accentuate the *RRR*, and they don't know the right order of the words!)

I already hear the fourth finch, he complains:

Want to beat me?

Another agrees:

Beat him ... beat him ....

It sounds like:

Even the serious woodpecker pecks like mad, and counts:

How much do I get ....

for this loving?
These lovers!

16.4.1922

# The three hens

[By the time that I knew Janáček there were only two hens: perhaps one had died. The remaining two had to jump on his table every night for his goodnight caress.

Anyone who saw this dear man as I did, in the evening of his days, sitting in his garden and communicating with his plants and animals, could not doubt where the strength of his music lay.

Some composers go into a faraway world for their inspiration. That in itself makes them neither greater nor less. It is simply one way of seeking inspiration. But Janáček loved the world of nature, of animals and of human beings, and observed their behaviour, and sound patterns more accurately and closely than any other composer. It is in these observations and his power of recording them, that his true greatness and originality are to be found.]

Their eyes were all the same: the pupils round, black, but the whites of the eyes yellowish; Mrs Kovalská's quite red, as if she had been crying.

For each of them the wattle and comb were blood red. In Mrs Bílá's case, both wattle and comb were minute, undeveloped; Mrs Slavkovská had a long wattle and Mrs Kovalská had a comb bent to one side.

She is really a fiery creature with a dash of the cock in her temperament.

When she came into the garden for the first time, she ran across like mad and ......crash! In the corner of the garden on the compost heap, half sitting, half lying, without a movement, she stayed for two hours!

Mrs Bílá has the gentlest nature. One can stroke and pet her.

You just tell her

Come on, sit down

and she settles herself.

Mrs Slavkovská is a fat granny. She is marvellously dressed in brown and black, with gold stripes! A solemn waddling walk, but silent. I have not caught yet one of her speech patterns. But she has serious thoughts. The other day, suddenly, a thrush flew in, looking for its lost little one, still without feathers or tail. Mrs Slavkovská ruffled her feathers and shrieking, chased her away.

Mrs Bílá occasionally drops a word, as if it were gold from the depth.

This is it

She philosophises.

It is strange, it sounds as if all three were stuttering. This usually happens with people who talk before their thoughts ripen!

Mrs Kovalská is like a living children's trumpet. She talks constantly and doesn't let anybody get a word in.

Her little comb on top of the ash-grey coat looks like fire on a roof. And how piercing is the sound of her words!

What! What is it?

(She pronounces her ''C's'' badly, making them hard, where they should be soft.)

All three of them walk deep in thought on the lawn, until they reach the rockery. A green lizard flashes by like lightning and disappears into the rockery. Terrifying vision! Slimy reptile!

Kovalská shouts

From the stretched neck of Mrs Bílá came the same motif;

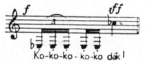

A warning to the whole hen population. They could not be calmed. Even during the afternoon siesta, the vision of the lizard terrified Mrs Kovalská. I turned when I heard the frightened sound she emitted during her dream.

BBBLOODD!

Another day! She started crying. It was full of pain and sounded like a premonition.

Oh, is this it? ....

Suddenly, a transition was heard, high in thin harmonics, like struggling beams of sunlight.

One day she ran around the garden, and jumped on the railing of the summerhouse. Suddenly she quietened down and disappeared.

Anxiously we looked for her.

And suddenly, look! Among the flowering lilies sat Mrs Kovalská and beside — her first egg!

From that time she changed her nature. She is much calmer.

Evening shadows fell on the garden. Onto my table first flew Mrs Bílá; Mrs Slavkovská with difficulty also succeeded. I stroke them both; they settle down, gradually their eyes close.

Mrs Kovalská runs doubtfully around.

Koko — I should like to

She thinks to herself "I'd like to join them". A bat flies around in the darkening shadows. That settles it! I am sitting and stroking Mrs Kovalská too.

That is how I tamed three hens. They respond to my call:

As you see, it is the most usual rhythm of their speech. They particularly like the call when I feed them. They really understand it.

We should understand each other better, if we spoke to each other in the same rhythm, melody and articulation!

With the child we talk baby language; with animals in an animal voice. "Pila, pila" the geese understand; "Čiči, Čiči" a pussy cat; "Vijo" a pony; "Kva, Kva", frogs.

24th June 1922.

# The little cockerel

The egg was first put under the broody hen in May. Three weeks later it was hatched, and on 18th September Mary called out:
"He has begun to sing!"

His territory is the yard, so small that I could jump over it; the henhouse with a little ladder up to the attic and a fruit garden densely carpeted with grass.

From there he can pass through a hole in the hedge — his gate — between vegetable beds into the flower borders which edge the yellow sanded paths.

Head down bent, he watches me with his left eye.

A fiery little comb, tall yellow little legs; in colour, ashen. His tail feathers five fingers in height.

What a long time he stands in this heroic posture!

The rest of the tribe (except for two fowl and a broody hen) are still chickens and are observing the unkempt heads of broccoli and the tilted heads of cabbage.

Suddenly the little cockerel roused himself from his thoughts, turns, dives downward and up again quickly, so as not to miss anything, stretches his little body, puffs up, his little beak opens, and immediately through the air flies his little song:

Ky - ki - ri ký -

The cocks of the farmers Strakoš, Nikl and Sobotik answer him. But they don't spoil each other's greetings. They always wait for the ending before they begin again their own angelus.

Night is drawing near. The sunshine slants towards the wooded hill, as if its circle of fire wanted to rest on the hill, and there it settles in a fiery sunset.

Before you begin to look for the unwelcome shadows which creep from the deep forest and steal the colour from the flowers, the green from the gardens, shadows which change the tops of the trees into black balls and transform them against the lighter sky into witches and monsters, — before you can see all this happening, the sun is already behind the hill. The people of Příbor have still a little sunshine. The yard has become quiet.

The last into the henhouse and on to the little ladder jumps the broody hen.

And on the perch?

Hens, chickens, black, speckled, whitish yellow, closely packed next to each other, pushing, throwing each other off, and straightening out again.

Suddenly the little cock catches the broody hen, the last one in, catches her by the crest, and makes unmistakable approaches.

"This has never happened to me before, that such a rascal should dare...." gasped the affronted broody.

The chickens are stretching their little necks with curiosity. It's a good thing that it's too dark for them to see.--

Good night!

I am closing the little door, for safety.

In the dark grey sky in the direction of Moravska Ostrava one can see the black outline of the tower of Rychaltice. On it the symbol of a cockerel. The wedge of the Babi mountain and the Hukvaldy castle project, forming a mysterious black cut-out; from it extends a net, which is full of glittering stars, shining silver in the grey, dark night. A child would love to paint it.

I remember too the little cemetery by the tower of Rychaltice, where my mother's heart lies.

Is it dawn already?

The quiet of the night was shattered by the tune.

Nine seconds pass, and again the cock calls,

Melancholy, veiled by the night, dying away.

And so six times in succession and then a long "no more."

It seems to me as if somebody mixes the darkness with heavy thoughts. It is such a painful silence.

Do you sing in your dream?

Ten times in succession the little cock crowed, always at longer intervals, the last one was fifteen seconds.

Ironically, into my mind came *Danse Macabre* by Saint-Saëns. And then out of Dvořák's *The Spectre's Bride.*

"Listen, suddenly nearby

The cock crows in the hamlet

And after him in the village

All the cock's companions

The dead, arose ....."

Ah, well, the end of the midnight comedy. I open the shutters — it is half-past four in the morning.

The little cock is awake from the first rays of the sun, and only when he has caught its last rays does he sleep.

And a little biblical history: "Amen, verily I say unto you that this day, even in this night, before the cock crows twice, thou shall deny me thrice."
This is how the little cock found his way into poetry!

They push his motif into music, and place a caricature of him on towers. The painter Jaronek stylises him as the Red Cock, and he flies through a flame on to the roof.

I am walking up Kounicova Street and from out of the dark cellar of the corner house comes the desperate sound of the cock! Not his happy; "kykiriky! But as if pincers were at his heart.

Is this the Bible story retold?

Surely Christ turned when he heard this cock's song:

" — as if with pincers at his heart he......?"

The old woman calls the geese:

*Pi - la   pi - la   pi - la   pi - la!*

At the speed of a second it sounded like the quiet cackle of geese.

Out of her fear for the little geese she called them with a motif which geese recognise, and to which they respond with understanding. The same psychological situation exists for animals as for man. They too recognise in sound the psychological course of composition.

These elements, reactions and perceptions are only an infinitesimal fragment of the whole range of composition.

Even if we add to our own dictionary of sound the richness of invention and fantasy, we still should not be able scientifically to classify a musical work.

So we haven't yet arrived either at a classification of musical science or a classification of the musical profession.

I am spinning together into a single thread the characteristics of a composer. I wind into this thread all accessible phenomena.

Today I entwine the little cock too in my ball.

Well, even Christ listened when he crowed!

# *Young Mr Starling*

[Dr M F Washbourne was a professor of philosophy and psychology in Vassar. In this article Janáček pokes fun at her scientific methods in dealing with bird life.]

Slender and black he balanced on the highest little branch of the plum tree. He looks all around him, and sometimes towards heaven. There, in a gliding flight of swallows, circle many Mr Starlings, Mrs and Miss Starlings too.

Why doesn't he go up and join them? What still holds him here on the bare top of the plum tree?

Now he waves and beats with his little wings against his little body, and drums with his little beak, as on a tambourine.

This is a prelude to a wedding flight, to a wedding song.
Now hardly audible, restrained:

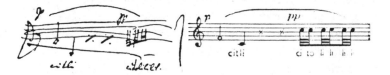

Three motifs, accompanied by the knocking of his little
beak, the waving of wings, clearly tuned and the ending as if
with a tiny little bell.

After a while he repeats it, and again a third time, and
soon he flies high up to join the gentlemen and ladies of his
own kind.

Psychology of animals, animal soul! *Mrs Washburn!*
Your research method: ''the way of experiment — let us
expose the animal — Mr Starling — to different influences,
which we are able to change, and let us observe how the
animal behaves — perhaps also a Miss Starling — under different conditions.''

— Here your method of reasearch will probably fail.

The starlings and their wives flew here recently, and soon
will fly away again. It is the 25th April, they circle in the
heights scanning the horizons of distant countries.

Suddenly one dropped, as if he fell onto the green lawn of
the garden.

Perhaps one ought to trap him and ''expose him to different influences!''

Oh no! Poor little thing, he would beat himself to death in the trap. One "influence" would be ascertained — his little soul would fly away.

"Psychological elements!" It is necessary to ascertain about these animals from their complete life-pattern, in full liberty and freedom of the animal — even of our Mr Starling.

From his life I have captured three of his motifs of expression, and they say a lot. They would hardly be likely to have been heard after these various "experimental influences".

1.5.1924.

# *The little goldfinch*

[From 1912 to 1926 Janáček kept in his house, adjoining the Conservatoire, a goldfinch, who was an exceptionally good singer. Then the bird went blind and died. The Mary mentioned, who forgot to feed the bird, was, for many years, a housekeeper to the Janáčeks.]

You are Spring's singer, you modest little goldfinch. At the edges of the forest, preferably in the thinnish bushes of the shallow rivers, among the stone fossils, richly embroidered by thistles, you flash like a live flower. In your flight you play with the rainbow and reflect its colours.

Everything around you is washed clean: the polished pebbles are warming in the sun, the sand is sparkling and on the lawn are diamond dewdrops.

You don't seek the sun, you love hiding in the dappled shade of the alder.

Down here, amongst us mortals, in the thistles of fate and the shadows of our daily turmoil, you sing comprehendibly for us a song of youth and spring. You don't fly away with your song into the blue sky, you don't lose yourself and your song in empty space like the skylark, with his defiant crest.

A pity perhaps that you haven't the legato song of the nightingale! Those birds who are so very, very exalted!

No! Have you seen how a white flower peels back the skin on a bud? Have you ever heard a simple little chicken peck until he breaks his shell? Have you lived through the storm of streams of new ideas? Ones which tear and destroy?

In the song of spring and youth there is no languor, no weakness or softness. Neither is there a subjugating power, no inexorably rigid direction. There is however a live force through which, although youth is aware of his vulnerability, he can ignore it. I think our bullfinch sang this song in paradise.

My little goldfinch, you squeaked. In longing, in the joy of life you have squeaked motifs intricate, complicated, hasty, in one breath — in ninety seconds — until our ears are buzzing. I could not detect the idea behind the song. Every little voice called ''Live, only live!''

I think that only when you were tired, and you perched, when your stomach called for food, only then did your motif have sense behind it. From then it was clear that you are aware that you can call for what you need.

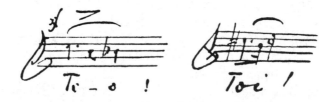

A little modesty was in these calls, repeated in the same way several times.

It was possible in this call to read a reproach to Mary, who was supposed to look after you:

(The colouring suggested "When will'ee? When will'ee?")

"Now, now" said the song, a request to pour some seed:

Three times repeated.

The tone of an ordinary conversation had these melodies:

always three times repeated.

The last one you could understand as: "Come on then, come on then, come on then!" — with an honest trill on the end.

The proper answer to Mary's call was:

Something has happened! The goldfinch is beyond himself, as if he sang in desperation.

Quite an unusual melody was heard, as if he wanted to say: "What is this?"

Tě - fo - i - ti  fo - i - ti  tě - te - je!

and again the same.

Every being quietens and stiffens when a foreboding of evil reaches him.

Little goldfinch, where is your playfulness? You used to lie on your back, and jerk the wires as if you played on the harp. You have forgotten all this. You were afraid of the water, but now you often dip your little head. You try to cure yourself.

In the spring sun suddenly he swiftly waved his wings for flight — but he could no longer raise himself even to the lowest perch.

Shrunk into a little ball, his head under his wing, he suffered.

That night he died.

Why so many words about a goldfinch's problematic melodies on the burning stone, on the prickly thistles, on the dew-spangled lawn? Firstly, I loved *him* or *her*. And also I am collecting suitable company for my *Cunning Litle Vixen*.

1.6.1921.

# Seven crows

A crow, black as old age, glided gently down the other day on to a branch of the nut-tree in my garden. The grass was already grey with frost, the fern was rusty, a few yellow leaves of the currant remained, silver-edged.

The nut-tree made his bed of fallen leaves; the bare little branches, like dirty little hands, still held, here and there, a few little nuts. The crow of course knew this.

Today on 8th November 1922 all was black on the nut-tree. Seven crows descended on it.

Clearly they had said to each other: ''There are enough nuts left for the whole family.''

Unfortunately I know only one word from their conversation:

I think they left out the second syllable: — du.

It ought to have been a bashful KRRRADU (I steal). But they were allowed to pick what nuts were left.

They picked, actually they threw them into my garden, from the highest branches, where we could not reach even by beating with a pole. They picked a full basket.

When, on 14th November they flew off, high into the sky, so high that I could hardly hear their cry of invitation:

It reminded me of the fairy tale. There they were not seven crows but seven brothers, transformed into crows by an evil spell, and somewhere their little sister was sewing magic clothes for them, made out of the red sky of evening.

When she has finished the sewing and throws the magic clothes over their shoulders, the curse on the crows will fall from them.

I really wanted to call after them:

"Do come again next year!
The little clothes will be ready."
But they flew away.

O, to gather into one's memory the rhythms of these coloured miracles — from the yellow currant leaves with silver edges to the nebulous silver of the quiet river Visla, over which they flew away!

To remember too, in painful silence, the gravelly, childish, innocent voice of a buzzard,

which hung in a pool of clouds!

To add to it the rhythm of agitated breathing, and the sad beat of a heart.

To be one with the crows.

In whatever rhythm, in whatever tempo they wound into their little brains the beauty of these pictures, in the same rhythm they are able to unwind them.

That is why the crows will return at the same time, into the same neighbourhood — and this will be the sixth year in succession.

Identical ripples of emotion compel rhythms of tone which accord with rhythms of colours and touch.

This is the secret of the conception of a musical composition, an unconscious spontaneous compilation in the mind.

By this symptom are composers initiated.

There would be no composers of genius if musicians didn't experience and enjoy the charm of rhythms recorded by eye, ear or touch.

And a composer's work, sounding like floating bubbles which emerge from perception — even if it runs wild with fantasy, nevertheless becomes a work of disciplined thought, like every scientific work.

In short.....

But what an uproar? As if clouds were colliding.

The seven crows have aleady returned!

Their little sister is wringing her hands.

She hasn't finished her sewing. How could she have collected so much of the red sky of evening!

But whatever she has been able to catch, she throws over the shoulders of the poor little crows.

Now how happily they shed their black feathers! But one breathlessly tries in vain to tear them from his right wing.

Oh, dear! His little garment didn't have a finished right sleeve!

And so the right wing was left to the composer.

He flourishes it victoriously. He flies up with his creative gift so high that it is a wonder that he isn't lost in the heavens; but he keeps a firm foot on the ground as well.

*Conclusion.* Unkind tongues say that it wasn't the little sister who sewed the clothes out of the red sky of eventide, but that it was an ordinary girl and that many a composer must be satisfied with only one quill from a crow.

30.11.1922.

# *When little birds go to sleep*

[All the place names mentioned are in the district of Luhačovice Spa.]

All the cuckoos of the forest greeting each other! You can hear it from every direction.

The one on the hill Vysoka Kamenna in a motif of complete contentment: (in five seconds)

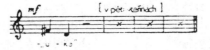

From the slopes of Obětava more grumpily:

On the Mala Kamenna he surely has a pain which calls for the waters of Luhačovice Spa:

He hasn't even finished and has to hurry away.
They all have the same call, and their melody has the same tempo.

It is half-past seven in the evening.

These tiny little birds have imbibed so much golden sunshine all through the day, that now their little heads and feet are wilting.

In the undergrowth before he sleeps someone still giggles:

Another holds his little tummy as he shakes with laughter:

And this one, on the highest shoot of the gay young fir to which he holds on, still tries out his ''sung in'' little throat with a trill:

The whole hillside of crickets make a ground bass for the music:

It sounded like a cripple in the nest making a yawning noise:

But the old finch got really angry: ''Can't we have peace?''

It is already high time to be quiet, hide and cuddle down!

Through the scented twilight of the forest a hungry, melancholy tone was heard:

.Cho-ho-ho-hó -

Even my sight sharpened to spy whether or not with a quiet, treacherous swoop the big-eyed owl wouldn't arrive.

The moon, innocently white, jumped over the tops of the trees, and looked into the birds' cradles.

The curled-up naked ones were already dreaming: in their dreams they opened their little beaks. The finch only blinked his little eyes.

But in the Slovakian Chalet there was a bird that didn't close his eyes. That bird was the American Indian, and his fiddle.....They were encouraged by the listeners to play indoors. There was a lot of giggling, and the audience became rather embarrassed.

Into the night the melancholy sound of the gypsy Indian's violin mixed with the heavy scent of the young forest.

All that was received by the bubbling stream. When it reaches you, perhaps it will tell you about the happiness of these quiet, carefree moments.

26.7.1927.

# GYPSY CHILDREN

## *They caught them*

[The two following memoirs belong to happenings in Pisek, a little Bohemian town, which Janáček often visited with his friend Kamila Stösslova. His devotion to her is transparently clear as she shows her compassion for the little gypsies and together they tried to help them.

As so often in these pages the apple-stealing recalls a similar episode in his own youth, when he was a child of the Cloister.]

You, who love the forest so much, but enjoy the hot beams of the sun on the rocks as well. You listen to the hunger of the fledglings in the nest; seven hungry throats!

They left the gypsy children in the woods. They captured the parents, but left the children to wander on their own.

See! You collect them; they follow you, you, yourself like a red flower.

See! In the streets of Pisek, by the river Otava, you lead them. What a vision!

When you reach home, unashamedly you strip them of their rags and clothe their nakedness with fresh underwear and your own children's clothes. They are dying of hunger, and you feed them!

See! Before the barred windows of the Pisek jail the children show themselves to their imprisoned parents.

See! "How nice we look. You, smallest of all, I want to keep. No, I want to go back to the forest!" shouts the child.

All want to give to the children!

And the children carry away food from the barred prison windows.

You, in whom Ostrovsky sought his Katya Kabanová; you, who Dostoyevsky would call the tortured soul of Akulka, and in whom I find the pure child's soul of Aljeja.

You, whom I do not want to name; you, who clothed and fed the gypsy children. They know you in Pisek there by the stream, and in every little cottage.

You lead sick old women into the sun and console and heal them with your words.

They caught all the gypsies in the forest of Pisek and shut them up cruelly in prison.

You caught their poor little children into your heart.

Which of the remedies, I wonder, will cure more quickly?

3.7.1927.

## For a few apples

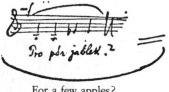

For a few apples?

The nurse pushed a girl, as thin as a hospital broom, into the next room. "Haven't I told you, you must not come into contact with other people!"

She banged the door behind her and looked through the little spyhole. The child was already sitting on the plank bed.

Oh, what are you writing again?

What am I writing? Go on, speak away.

My God, bed bugs, stifling air, lice crawling on to the children's bodies — locked up in the next room.

What have you done? Why did they shut you up?

Listen, Guvnor

I have pinched apples too, said the girl.

*Na vinici jsem je trhala.*

I picked them in the vineyard

But I didn't pick them; I was only holding and bending down a well-laden branch for the boys, when from nowhere the owner appeared.

"Whose brat are you? Come on down!"

"Not likely!" The branch creaked and I climbed higher. "If you want me, come on up!" The boys vanished as if they had sunk into the ground.

"But I know you, you black imp! I shall settle with your father!"

As he went, the branch creaked again.

Home I flew like the wind.

Those few apples cost a box on the ears, and a gulden.

But "listen Guv'nor" for a few apples they have imprisoned five gypsy children for the third day.

I, too, have pinched somebody else's apples.

We are crawling under a little bridge — you couldn't get into the monastery garden by the path. Under the bridge all is cobwebs and darkness.

At lunchtime when we went for water, we had seen the heavily-laden trees. At night it was difficult to locate them. The branch broke and....

"Thieves!" shouted Father Alip from his window on the first floor.

We leapt over fences and through the cloister to escape!

In the doorway with a lighted candle held high stood our Director Pavel Křižkovsky!

As reluctantly, one after the other we had to pass him, a minor scale was played on us.

For a few apples in our pockets, a minor scale in every octave. I got a slap on the face in the highest octave.

Since then I ask everybody, and I hear that everyone has committed this childish sin of pinching apples, climbing over somebody's garden fence to pick — pick — forbidden fruit!

In the hospital at Písek there is a garden. Little red apples smiled at our five gypsy children.

The tallest one picked one for each of them.

For this they put all five of them into that dismal den and shut them up.

The day after tomorrow their mother is supposed to come for them. They caught the parents, and imprisoned them for weeks and weeks, but they didn't find any proof of guilt.

At the gate of the hospital five gypsy children waited for their mother, and when they could wait no longer they all went to sleep on the pavement.

Does this, dear lady, make it any easier to say farewell to them?

Luhačovice, 4.9.1927.

# TRAVEL

## *The sea, the earth*

[This article is about Janáček's visit to England from 28th April to 10th May 1926, and to Berlin from 29th to 31st May 1926.

On the return journey he went through Germany to Holland, and from Vlissingen by boat to Folkestone.

Adela Fachiri was an English violinist, of Hungarian birth, who gave the first performance of his Violin Sonata in England.

Prof. Dent and Rosa Newmarch were among the first pioneers of his music in England.

Janáček refers to Mr Oscar Bie, a German critic, who wrote an unfavourable review of the Berlin performance of *Katya Kabanova* in *Lidové Noviny*, the Brno paper for which Janáček wrote these articles.]

Into the deep furrow dug by our ship fall masses of dark-green sea water hemmed with white, thick foam. Our direction, Vlissingen — Folkestone is crossed every few minutes by a brightly-coloured cargo steamer.

On the flat horizon, as far as one can see, suddenly a black fishing boat with sails appeared.

She stopped.

As if through her the sea became entangled with sadness and melancholy.

Nothing is easier than to express in music storms, mountains, sunrise — and to be satisfied with these simple expressions.

How easily this music lies upon the bed of space, with zigzag lightnings, and the thunderings of nature!

On the limitless surface of the sea our mood becomes indifferent. Even the tempo of our thoughts calms down; speech, facial expression, even our steps get slower.

Even music dies away.

And without resistance, unconsciously, these symptoms steal into the production and reproduction of a composition.

Broad areas of space conjure up in the mind great stretches of time, and broad diffused areas of emotion. It is through this experience that I can understand the clinging to the musical past, the conservative element in the English musical mind.

Just as the sea erodes here and builds up there — so similarly is formed the musical character of the English and the Nordic nations.

And the cold and the yellow fogs reinforce the effect of the sea.

It is possibly these factors which result in the correctness of English bowing, the breathing of the windplayer, and the touch of the pianist.

Their whole mind is occupied with measurement, they differentiate the correct shades of the tempo, equally they trim the flame of emotion.

But it is not by holding on to measured areas, be they musical, or sometime those of colour or of thought but by breaking them, that one strikes emotional warmth.

Even the greatest beauty of tone feels cold if the artist has not the strength to break it — or if not to break it, to boil over — even if not dying, to burn — even if not to burn, to hurry — even if not to hurry, to exaggerate.

And just such an artist was Miss Adila Fachiri, a niece of

Joachim, playing my violin sonata. In my suite *Mladi (Youth)* and the quartet inspired by Tolstoy's *Kreutzer Sonata*,

the smile was dying,
the joke became serious,
the terror didn't frighten,
the passion didn't boil.

In all of them there was a barrier. *The sea.*

Not to stiffen — not to boil over — not to die down — not to burn — not to exaggerate is also the emotional lot of the listeners. They are satisfied with mediocrity of execution, satisfied with light which contains no ray of sun. Satisfaction not from fire and flame but from a fireside glow: equally they fear a steep ascent and a storm of emotion!

I am standing fearlessly on the ship's deck; she sways at an angle of 45° from side to side. She plunges in her prow as if she wanted to stand on her head at the bottom of the sea. Waves rugged with foam beat on her sides. They shriek.

Out of the unending sea the storm has blown hills and valleys of water. The sun, with a half-closed eye, whipped up golden lightning on the surface of the water.

Like moles the passengers crawled into the friendlier entrails of the ship. My companion lies asleep in the cabin. So few people witness this miracle of nature. So many of the artistic community evade the vitalising influence, not only in blossoming and peace, but also in nakedness and fury.

But in England I found an open heart and mind in Professor Dent and Mrs Rosa Newmarch.

I am standing on the beach at high tide. Ever-increasing waves are mounting, higher and higher. Each one roars his motif:

This one seethes:

This one yells:

It seems to me that all these motifs tumble over each
other, crash into one another anxiously swelling the impor-
tance of each other. The white foam spits furiously. I don't
realise that I myself am standing in this hungry foam. As it
is thrown onto the pebbles and rocks the afternoon sun has
burnt its silver mantle into a grey mourning shroud.

Something mysterious, which lifts this enormous mass of
sea, day by day, at the same time awakens also a tide in me. I
should like to embrace this wonderful vision of nature!

The gates of Vlissingen waterlock have closed. Many sea
creatures flowed into the lock. Among them a lot of little

monsters, in the shape of a four-eyed pretzel, made of blue or white dough. A translucent veil emerges from their bodies and dips and lifts coquettishly, they wind and unwind. They roll over like skilled swimmers — silently.

Already we have been journeying for three hours, through sand and pastures and pine groves on ground as flat as a floor.

The people have trusting faces, which are ready to smile, but the smile is checked at the strange sound of our speech.

I am in Berlin, where I am understood, and they say that this city is interested in my work!

No, Mr O. Bie! There was no bark of the German oak tree over *Katya Kabanova* on 31st May 1926, neither did the stage smell like a Bavarian brewery. The softness, the lyricism of the work with its dramatic accents, which arrested even our heart beats, was preserved. The hidden scent, the meadows in flower, the silent nostalgia and the moan of the wide Volga, were easily conjured up on the broad stage.

The performances were executed exactly according to the instructions in the score. All the notes became alive with joy; they all had their time and space. In the same emotion that they originated, in that emotion they subsided. They searched and found every little root in the work and saw that it shouldn't dry up but grow in sound and joy.

Katya descends to the fateful meeting. The conductor let Katya's trembling footsteps fall in utter silence, both in the orchestra and on the stage. The silence became so tense that it was like the pulsation of a ripe ear of corn. A pulsation of quivering silence.

And how the storm rages in the third act from the orchestra of 95 players. Such performances are dazzling and open wide the gates of the whole world to this work.

We are all here; Schreker and Schönberg, Kleiber and Zweig, Jeritza, Jurjevskaja and Helmova and a row of others beside. We are all fed by the sea of colour and shapes, the sounds which fill the air, the cheerful sky, the fertile joyful earth.

When from behind the hill the silver moon arises, we meditate to the sound of a nocturne; when at the foot of a mountain the river winds in another direction, the storm dies down — we resist with the counterpoint; with the little skylark we sing a song; we climb the slopes of a mountain; we revel in motifs as in a flowery meadow; the chords harden for us like nuts, and at other times they spread and shine like blue mist on a mountain, as long valleys join to form the countryside; in this way our work is knitted together.

We know that tomorrow the blue flower will fade, the pine tree will grow taller — we rejoice in the beauty of to-day, we know that the morrow will hold another beauty. Here on Mother Earth we are children of progress. Even in my music we are dependent on her.

When I remember the events in London from 29th April to 11th May, in Berlin from 29th—31st May — here within reach of my hand two little birds stretch their bare little necks from the nest. The parents fly, hesitatingly from the fence to the gutter, from the rosebush on to the spreading apple tree.

"To fear or not to fear?"

"No fear!"

And with a long green caterpillar in their little beaks they fly in to the nest, to their little ones.

And to this philosophy of life also belongs

my voice

Hukvaldy, 10.6.1926

[This is an account of Janáček's visit to London by Jan Mikota who accompanied him.]

On 30th April 1926 there appeared in the Times this very short notice:

> Mrs Rosa Newmarch is giving a small reception this afternoon at Claridge's to welcome the Czechoslovak composer Dr Leoš Janáček.

This English woman, Mrs Newmarch, is a friend of the Czech nation, who has visited Czechoslovakia several times and met Czech artists and learnt to love particularly the works of Leoš Janáček. After Anton Dvořák, Leoš Janáček is the second Czechoslovak composer to be invited to England to be present at concerts of his own compositions.

On the initiative of Mrs Newmarch a group of prominent musicians was formed to organise Janáček's visit to London. This English woman first arranged a small party to which she invited English artists, publishers and music critics to meet Janáček. Maestro Janáček was very excited, wondering how it would all go. Would the guests really turn up? The day before he had been welcomed at the railway station by the Czechoslovak ambassador, Jan Masaryk and by Czechs living in London, but these were, after all, his own people.

But the question was how he could break through to the English people.

The result was wonderful. So many guests came and Janáček received so many invitations that he would have had to stay at least another fortnight to accept them all. On Sunday 2nd May the Maestro was taken by car to the summer home of the famous conductor Sir Henry Wood.

Janáček devoted himself wholeheartedly to the preparation of the concert. He did not miss a single rehearsal and

Mrs Rosa Newmarch, Mme Adila Fachiri, Janáček, Mr Fachiri and Miss Fanny Davies — a photograph taken in London in 1926

Janáček and Sir Henry Wood — London 1926

after his explanations the English artists were even more in love with his works.

The programme was: String Quartet No. 1 (1923), Violin Sonata (1921), the suite for six wind instruments called *Youth*, and *Fairy Tale* for cello and piano (1910). The concert was an enormous success, unending applause and calls for the composer, who, very moved, thanked the artists and the audience from the platform.

Janáček's letter from London to his friend Mrs Kamila Stössel. (The strike referred to is the General Strike of 1926).

> My dear Mrs Stössel!
>
> If I were to continue living like this I should certainly be dead in a month. Nothing but parties, food and sailing round in cars all day! There is a strike on. The Londoners nearly missed their milk this morning. Prices go up and up. It is a bad atmosphere for a concert. But I have succeeded in what I set out to do. I have made many friends and found a patron who says that *Jenufa* will be performed within a year. Now I must return home otherwise I fear I might never get away from here.
>
> Yours very sincerely
>
> > Leos Janáček Ph.D.
> > London 5th May 1926

# A few words from a holiday in Russia

*Petrograd 26 July 1896*

Do you want a picture of Petrograd? Imagine Prague. Bond Street with Ferdinand Avenue are like Neva Prospect (Trafalgar Square), through which, from early morning until late at night, life runs overflowingly. From left and right into this main street lead neighbouring streets. Ligorska Avenue cutting through Nevsky Prospect from the east has a working-class character. A lot of factories and big establishments of every variety. In the middle of the street, previously the Ligorski Canal, along the whole length is a row of shady trees, in three places broadened into children's parks. What a lot of these little darlings play here in the sand! Here they are completely safe, because the children's parks are surrounded by a thick iron fence, so that not even a dog can attack the children. What wonderful protection for the safety of the worker's children. On both sides of the avenue of trees are noisy thoroughfares paved with cobbles and the pavements are paved with flagstones. The cleanliness throughout the whole length is exemplary, because every householder is responsible for the brushing and watering of the street in front of his house, up to the middle of the road. A hydrant is set in the pavement in front of each house. The road can be very quickly watered and swept.

One more health precaution I like in this worker's street: in front of every public house there is a barrel filled with water which has been boiled and cooled. Nobody drinks any other water. It is the duty of the publican always to provide fresh, cooled water for the thirsty pedestrian, and the local

policeman strictly supervises this. You don't feel that you
are in a worker's street because all the signs of squalor that I
remember from some Brno streets don't exist here.

Next in interest comes the navigable Fontanka Canal,
which cuts through the Nevsky Prospect and boasts of exceptional activity. All the way from Warsaw one saw enormous stores of birchwood. Now we can see where they were
being sent. An unending stream of rafts, 20 to 40 metres
long, nailed together by boards and beams with wooden
pegs, and filled with short cut logs for burning, is anchored
along the whole length of the Fontanka. There is hardly
enough room for the little steamers to weave in-between.
Steamers which busily negotiate passenger transport between the beaches of the mainland and the islands. The
wooden rafts are anchored there until all the wood is sold.
Then they dismantle even the rafts and sell everything that
is burnable. Electricity works are anchored in the Fontanka,
and also markets for live fish.

We shall disregard some crossing streets and canals. (The
best known for its breadth is the Moyka). The golden pin-
nacle which towers to heaven tells us that we are near the
River Neva.

The Admiralty lies, as it were, in about the same position
to the Nevsky Prospect as the National Theatre to the Ferdinand Avenue in Prague. It is a quadrangle of big buildings.
Walking through the park on the right-hand side we see an
unsuspected vista of great beauty. We are standing on the
left bank of the Neva, by the palace bridge. On our right-
hand proudly rises the Winter Palace of the Czars. Beyond
the dark blue surface of the Neva towers the Peter and Paul
Citadel; the golden tower of the cathedral of the same name
marks the burial ground of the Czars, Princes and
Princesses of Russia. In front, to the right of the water's
edge, stand two lighthouses: to the left are several islands, of
which Jelagin is the most attractive.

You surely perceive quite a similarity between the panorama from the Charles Bridge in Prague and the Palace Bridge in Petrograd. Here of course it is all in larger proportion — on the islands are towns, and to cross the Trojicky Bridge takes 800 steps. Petrograd faces Europe with five streams of the Neva; the most southern is the River Neva; then to the north follow "little River Neva", "little Nevka", and finally "the great Nevka".

Near the Admiralty is the harbour for steamships, which float towards the fortress of Kronstat, as well as to the summer residence of the Czar — to Peterhof.

Let us take a steamer, which will leave in a few minutes to the latter destination. We steam into the bay and on the left are five heroic battleships. The horizon of the bay widens, looking as if silver was spilt over the enormous area which disappears into the distance of the sky. Petrograd behind us falls into the slightly rippling, lead-coloured surface of the water. To the left and to the right we meet passenger ships navigating. On the horizon are a few big sailing ships. Look, here returning from Peterhof is the delegation from Korea! Unattractive-looking people in long, loudly coloured gowns. Sea birds fly from buoys, red, which are anchored and are used to mark the route.

We are in the Bay of Finland. I am the second who will bring into the little village of his birth waters from the Baltic Sea. The first was Jan Čapek from San and Hukvaldy, a Hussite Captain.

*Petrograd 30 July 1896*

At the end of the Nevsky Prospect on the south-east is a monastery, where theology is taught on a high level.

The main cathedral, which houses the relics of St Ivan Nevsky, is just being repaired. The coffin radiates with silver, and so do the surroundings which are full of pious pilgrims. A similar picture to St Johns in Prague. In the extensive gardens the church singers conglomerate; children and grown-ups, dressed in dark-blue cassocks, belted around the hips and banded with gold.

In a side chapel of the cathedral, on the first floor, at 11 in the morning, a panychida (Requiem Mass) is celebrated. A small, light chapel with a parquet floor. In the back stand the deceased's relatives, in the front the ceremony begins. It is well known that the Russian choirs are excellent, and, believe me, for a musician it was a pleasure to listen to. The ceremony, from a musical point of view, is compact; the choir joins in the responses with admirable lightness. These always end with a long murmuring pianissimo, and the priest, with a perfectly intonated note, continues the prayer. No interruptions, no stops, no strident modulations. The musical element does not draw attention to itself and doesn't distract the mind from the ceremony. The gentle sound, almost a muted sound of the choir, contrasts well with the full-sounding voice of the priest....From that moment I am sure of one thing, that the roar of the German mixtures, fifths, cornets, etc., on our organs are blasphemous.

From the quiet corner of the monastery, the town railway takes us into the turmoil of life in the Nevsky Prospect. The local train goes so slowly that you can jump on and off whenever you want. From the Nikolajev Square into the city's bustle there are no more trains; they are replaced by a horsedrawn car, which, for an inclusive fare of 5 kopeks, takes you for more than an hour's journey.

But to complete the life of the Nevsky Prospect is Izvostik, the cabby. Sitting on the box of his light little coach he urges passers-by with his full voiced ''Please, would you like?'' untiringly. He asks for one rouble, but he also will take 20 kopeks. On his head he wears a little black hat, with the top cut straight down, a dark blue kaftan tied around with a gaily-coloured belt. No whip is to be seen. The horse, hollow-backed, well fed, usually black with a long tail, gallops through the street, but the cabby is in complete control, the reins in both hands. I have seen as high a number as 1400 on the cab, although most of the cabbies leave Petrograd in the summer to serve in the surrounding summer residences. The Izvostik is always at hand; for reasons of cleanliness he is not allowed to feed the horse in the street. There are special yards for feeding horses to which the cabbies drive. From early morning, right through the night, he drives from place to place, because he has no definite stand or rank, and he is trying to earn a living. The cabby is the same everywhere, in Petrograd as in Moscow or Nižny Novgorod — and in all Russian towns. How advantageously different he looks compared to the cabby of Warsaw! In this sea of single-yoked troikas the silver glitters. The heads of the horses, as if they smelt something in the distance, held high, the tails streaming out. I now believe that a winged horse can be a picture of ascending flight. The width of the Nevsky Prospect is surely as wide as the Wenceslas Square in Prague.

There are a lot of shop-windows, stores, different goods. Do I see a store of Bohemian glass from the glass works of Count Harrach? So it is not Czech glass? Only the other day I drank at the bar Bohemian beer. Even Pilsner is here from the brewery in Riga. A bottle, a little less than half-a-litre, with a golden vignette, like those on bottles of the most precious wines, costs a mere 35 kopeks. The better restaurants are usually on the first floor; the menu always hangs in the passageway of the restaurant, so that one can decide where one would like to lunch.

I drank tea at eight in the morning. A cold meal of ham, hard boiled eggs, fish, etc., with tea, one eats around 10 o'clock. "Lunch" is prepared about 5 o'clock in the afternoon. Supper, usually tea with lemon, is drunk about 11 or 12 at night.

So in Petrograd one only eats to satisfaction once a day. The servants don't need to run from shop to shop because all spices, salt, greengrocery, meat, poultry, eggs, butter, etc. for the cooking are found under one roof. All this is found in one shop, the butcher. One buys more cheaply in the big Market halls, in the centre of the town. Beef and bread are sold at a fixed price. A Russian loaf of bread weighing a pound costs 3 kopeks. A worker needs to earn 20 kopeks so that he can have enough beef and bread. Our housewives will be interested in the price of our hare. It is more expensive by 10 kopeks than the Siberian white hare which can cost less than 15 kopeks. Yet the ''mužik'' delights in a raw cucumber, which he gobbles up, green skin and all. ''Mužik'' — I am not a Mužik: I am a Christian'', a worker answers you, if you would address him as ''Mužik''. This name is understood to mean a wretched fellow with ragged clothes, but not yet a beggar.

On the Nevsky Prospect the white military cap, white cloth of the officer's coat with gold buttons dominate. The ladies are in Paris dresses.

You will know the picture I am going to describe. It is the same as in our village. It is after Mass, the people stream out of the cathedral, where it is still hazy with incense. They group around the village cross. Nobody wants to go home because they only see each other on this occasion once a week! The same happens in front of the Catholic Cathedral on the Nevsky Prospect. They, too, only see each other once a week. And still they can't praise God in the same song! Here a Frenchman, a Pole, an Italian, a German. The latter, it seems to me, is on top. He is the organist who hadn't enough ideas for the voluntary; he needed it to last for the whole Mass, so in the end he played the German National Anthem.

## Petrograd 31 *July* 1896

What entertainment is there in Petrograd? It is 11th July
and we are going to the Zoological Gardens. It is next to the
Peter & Paul citadel. The cathedral is still open. The
Military Guard leads us politely from tomb to tomb. They
are of plain white marble, a metre high, and at their head
simple inscriptions, "Peter I", "Catherine II", "Nikolaj
I", "Alexander III", etc. No more inscriptions; no
boasting verses. The idea strikes me how curious it is that in
the history school-books in our middle schools that in all the
centuries of the development of this enormous empire you
won't find more than a simple picture of Peter I. It is that
which built the empire and holds it together — it must have
the strength of iron, and a heart of oak. We should know the
ideas through which they became victors, overcoming the
storms.

To return — what entertainment is there in Petrograd? A
great performance is announced in the Zoological Gardens.
Already at 4 o'clock in the afternoon the Military Band of
146th Infantry Regiment of the Czar is playing. At 5.30 the
animals are fed. At 6 o'clock there is a comedy in the
theatre, followed by a performance of *The Rubber Sisters
Janic*. After that comes the clown, Tom Felix, etc. etc. All
for the eyes and ears of the children, large and small. At the
same time on the vast, roomy verandah, which seats 2,000
people at tables, a complete orchestra is playing (from the
stands gazed out the eight long necks of double basses), conducted by Franke. The programme announced compositions
by Beethoven, Reinecke, Wagner and Delibes.

In the second part of the theatre was a farce, *The Corrupt
Innocents*. After that there were again a few new Russian
and English clowns. Franke's orchestra played again further
compositions by foreign composers.

In the third part was ballet, *In the Land of the Eternal Ice*:
eight scenes, of which the fifth was excellent — the ascent of

a balloon to find the Nansen ship, Fram. I couldn't believe that in a theatre with an open-air audience it was possible to produce so many lighting effects. The ballet, in which there are 200 people, was played about a hundred times. The sudden return of Nansen must have ruined the calculations of the Director, Alexej.

Mr Franke finished the third part of the entertainment with a new selection of foreign composers: the compositions had titles ''Banditenstreiche'', ''Der Obersteiger'', ''Santanella'', ''In Companiefront'', ''Golden Rain''. It is 12 o'clock....a magical night, warm and clear, like in our own country when it is cloudy. There are still a lot of the audience in the park. I am amazed. Perhaps next time I shall hear something more worthwhile from Mr Franke.

Since 11th July, the two Germans, Rost and Franke have not improved. The programme again shows Nicolai, Schubert, Ernst, Wagner, Kuken, Liszt and Mendelssohn! The Russian composer, Glinka, is only represented by two numbers.

''By nature a wall has been given by fate. It is necessary to make a window into Europe'', says Peter the Great in Pushkin's poem, *Petrograd*. Through this window so much foreign matter was squeezed that now even we Czechs are starting to use it, being historically connected to Russia. This year they closed the German Theatre, and the conducting of the magnificent concerts at the Pavlovsky Station has been entrusted to Mr Galkin, Professor of the Conservatoire in Petrograd. Before, they were conducted by Mr Strauss from Vienna. A return railway ticket, bought at the Pavlovsky Station, also entitled you to listen to these concerts, which of course are not of the same character every day. One day in the week is dedicated entirely to Russian composers; every Friday there is a big Symphony Concert.

On 12th July, by the Russian calendar, there was the eighth Symphony Concert in memory of Anton Rubinstein.

The following extensive works by that composer were
played:

1. *Ivan the Terrible*, a musical picture
2. Second Concerto for 'cello and orchestra
3. Songs
4. Fourth Piano Concerto
5. All movements of the Fourth Symphony

The musical picture, *Ivan the Terrible*, is a voluble piece;
luckily it was brilliantly played. In the 'Cello Concerto I like
the third movement, with its national idiom. Also in the
Piano Concerto Rubinstein exults with "the voice of the
people", and it remains "God's music". Mr Edward
Žakobo (Jacobo), the 'cello virtuoso, played cleanly and
quietly. What's the good of freezing beauty? I want to hear
progress in every tone, to know that he didn't go through it
with his finger muscles, but also through the fire in his
heart. In the last movement of the Piano Concerto arose a
disagreement between Gollidej, the piano virtuoso, and
Galkin, the conductor. I realise that my advice comes too
late, but the conductor should have conducted the 2/4 bar in
one beat, and Gollidej should have realised that one finishes
a piece in strict tempo together.

We have been listening already since eight o'clock; it is
after ten. The train, which should take us back to Petrograd,
is already breathing heavily quite near us. But one can't
depart without hearing the symphony: the excellent orchestra was a guarantee that it will be well played. Already
the second whistle, and they are only playing the Adagio,
the third movement. Finale — Largo. I am listening with
only half my soul and while on the run! The end, and
behind me the applause, roars like a storm.

Would you believe that in all the haste and hurry to find
even the last seat on the overcrowded train, a Czech found
me and recognised me. A countryman, at that time a
member of Galkin's exemplary orchestra.

At 12 o'clock we were again satisfied and elated in Petrograd. Who makes up the concert audience? All the intelligentsia from around, who meet together here. I should say there were 1,500 — 2,000 people in this well-ventilated hall. Here, the Russian intelligentsia were represented. With satisfaction I acknowledge that in the light entertainment parks it is mainly foreigners who take their pleasure. I should like to know and describe how the Russian people entertain themselves.

# *Basta!*

# *Venice: location of the 3rd Festival of Contemporary Chamber Music*

## (3rd—8th October 1925)

A city where kings should live — kings of the spirit. And they *did* live in Venice. Here the open sea narrows into the Grand Canal. Before the sea left, its white foam hardened into marble on little window decorations, on slim pillars, on smiling little statues, and symbolic statues, on palaces which line the water's edge.

With innumerable little tributaries, like the tentacles of an octopus, the sea winds itself around the city's proud buildings. Everywhere is a movement as of waves. This rocking movement does not stop, even at the height of the highest cathedral cupolas, nor on the highest edges of the Doge's Palace, nor on the calendar clock.....it only quietens when it reaches the blue vault of the sky.

All is quiet. The city stands as in a dream. Creative life is at a standstill, seeing only the creations of an ancient past.

You step into the Cathedral Chiesa dei Frari, and over-whelmed by its size you are unable to grasp its limitless space. You stand before the picture of the Assumption of Our Lady and you are convinced that the Mother of God ascends from it into the clouds. The pictures in the halls of the Doge's Palace speak of the events of history, and I feel the pictures should not be bounded by frames.

It is clean here. No noisy carriage wheels grind the stones to dust, and in the streets there are no cattle. Only four golden horses, and they are on the facade of St Mark's Cathedral. Even the shimmering surface of the lagoon is clean.

I return from my stroll through the city to my lodgings — Pensione Garbizza Saint Gregorio Fondemento Soranzo 335. I stumble out of the gondola into a little street, where by stretching out your arms you can touch the wall on the other side. The church "della Salute" dominates that quarter of the city. You hurry over a few little bridges which are humped over the canal and ultimately you are in your room. The floor, the bed is rocking with you. You open the window to enjoy the balmy summer air. From somewhere in the yard a song with indistinguishable words is heard:

In steals a mosquito — a gypsy, and sings right in your ear his blood-thirsty nocturne:

You listen angrily, but nevertheless fall asleep.

This is the only city that could have been chosen for a festival of modern music. Nevertheless, a warning! The history of music has been written into the archives of Venice. The names of Willaert (born 1490), Zarlino, Andrea and Giovanni Gabrielli, Giovanni dala Croce, and Marcello, and in our day Verdi and Wagner. From there, the golden thread of the development of composers wound itself to include Hasler of Prague, and Gallus of Olomouc. Bound by the same golden thread are Scarlatti, P.E. Bach, Haydn and Mozart. On today's ladder of fame are the names of 28 composers. In comparison with the works of these geniuses of the past we were given the unworthy trifles, which were played for five evenings in the luxurious La Fenice Theatre.

Just by speaking Czech!

Hotel de la Ville and not a room to be had! It is nearly midnight, and we are looking in vain for a room among the hotels in Trieste. In an overcrowded hotel somewhere right outside the city, anxiously we discuss what to do. The hotel maid offers us her own flat.

We reach the Via Enrico Totti by car; climbing four floors we find the room and are welcomed in Czech by Mrs Millič — a happy surprise!

The next day we see on the quayside two proud French military ships, and we follow the brisk commercial activity. We still have to wait for the train to Venice to leave.

At lunch: ''Have you a Czech waiter?''

''The Czech waiter left only yesterday! He was redundant. The Czechs always speak German''.

Do these Czechs realise for whom they make the mill turn?

People of Lachia

The Grand Canal is long and broad, but today you could cross from one side to the other with dry feet, gondola upon gondola huddled side by side across the canal. The Regatta and the race are in honour of the Duke of Aosta. The red gondola wins! Can it be only by water that he is carried? The roar droned like a waterfall, passionate shouts mixed into it like lightning. In this torrent was a gondola with sails. And it won!

An Italian, looking at me with ecstasy, ''This is a Venetian regatta!''

In the same spirit one listened in the Theatre Fenice. Basta! Basta! Enough! Enough! they shouted at Schnabl's *Sonata*. They laughed and whistled at the angel trumpets (Charles Ruggles). But a well-known German critic relieved his feelings in the Schönberg *Serenade* by shouting ''Berlin oaf!''

And yet I like these festivals of modern music!

Try shouting at Nature in the Spring — ''Don't grow''.

Basta! Basta! In vain they can shout against these festivals: still I can hear that in them the development of music continues to grow.

On St Mark's Square somebody calls after us

Addio Czechoslovaki!

8.11.1925

# The alarm bell rings

A rusty bell in the Bertramka.

The rust crept down the handle, and now it is broken off.

You little bell of around 1780! You used to call the family to meals, but now you ring in alarm.

Up a broken-down staircase, through a glass-covered passage to the rooms in which, hosted by the Dušek family, lived Mozart in the year 1787.

Cosy little rooms they are, everything in them gentle and small. Look, a cast of Mozart's ear above the hearth!

But the opera, *Don Giovanni*, called for a stony background under a wide sky, in the open air, close by the fountain. He had to see himself mirrored on its smooth surface, to direct his vision to the wooded hills of far-off distances. Now, you stony hand of the Commandatore, clasp the hand of the debauched Don Juan!

Clasp it! Roar with anxiety and pain, you trombones in the score!

On these little footpaths we walk in fear, evading the trail of earlier footsteps so that we don't disturb the shadows in the garden.

The ceiling would have fallen in. The water would have flooded the rooms. The windows would have rotted.

Mrs Emma Popelka has given this precious building as a gift to the Salzburg Mozarteum.

Three more years of their administration and this memorable building would be a ruin!

What is this?

Listen!

The bell jangles furiously. Ah, it is not a human hand that shakes it! It is the neglected memory of a genius who makes the accusation!

My dear lady, do you know that Mozart lightheartedly rang this little bell?

Could he ever have dreamed that this bell will shout the shame and the miserliness of the natives of Salzburg?

They now ask the Mozart Society in Prague for compensation to restore this property, this memorable building, the Bertramka.

343,000 crowns.

Would you believe it?

Three hundred and forty-three thousand crowns!

20.5.1928

# *Strolling*

## (Prague 5, 6, 7 January 1927)

The valley of the red deer

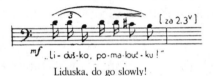

*mf* „Li-duš-ko, po-ma-louč-ku!"

Liduska, do go slowly!

It's impossible to go slowly! Liduška hops and skips so quickly because she wants to see the shaggy bear.

From a distance the eagle-owl warns her with his hollow hooting,

Ú-ú-ú!

but nothing bad happens.

Liduška runs down the steep snow-covered footpath and is already standing by the pit. On the other side are two shaggy bears. They lovingly lick the white snow with their little red tongues, as if it were honey.

The lord of the deep, dark forests, and now here he blinks with his eyes downcast, tailless, in a shed, imprisoned by wire!

The herds on the pastures of the High Tatra feared him, and now he sharpens his claws on the asphalt floor! No black earth, no soft moss. No thickets in which to scratch his fur, no snowdrifts in which he can roll to clean it.

They are imprisoned here for the pleasure and the fear, the awe and the dread that the children feel when they see them.

At All Saints.

At the altar of All Saints stand eight vested prelates, and in the choir gallery the organ is ashamed of the squeal of the fourth:

and of the bagpipes:

and they were surely ashamed of the chords by which they were accompanied.

The inquisitive English and French, who were there by accident, will certainly remember that somersault of a modulation at the end of the voluntary.

The Street.

As from the boundless deep of the sea, the town rises from the mist. First the little steeples appear piercing the dawn. Now it is gilded by the sun. One descends from the quiet of Petřin Hill; and soon the street sounds shout at one.

A yelling, whistling, panting, squeaking, creaking circle of noise surrounds you.

Into the indescribable turmoil we spill our conversation, Dr V. and I. We both cover our ears. Dr V is going-to-a-mee-ting-about the-state-taking-over-the-thea-tre!

We look at each other and immediately the counterpoint of the street divides us as might a wall.

The cloud of the tone

suddenly pierced by the shrieking sound

and bangs

In the distance a motor-car bangs, as it engaged in a fight,

and the horn of the Red Cross car doesn't presage anything good.

Oh, God! One is still missing! Over the uneven cobbles trundle the wooden wheels:

Under the silvery cover of the icy surface only the Vltava is silent.

16.1.1927.

# OPERATIC STUDIES

## Mr Brouček's excursion

*One to the moon, the other into the XV century*

[In this article, written in 1917, Janáček expresses his discontent with Czech materialism and complacency under Austrian domination. By means of satire he attempts to awaken nationalism in the Czechs. He tries to show them that they live on the moon and should return to the XV century to revive the great spirit shown by the Czechs in that age.

Svatopluk Čech (1846-1901) was a great Czech poet, and Janáček based his libretto on his nationalistic ideas.]

We are aware of many Broučeks in our nation — as many as there are Oblomovs in the Russians'. My idea was that we should abhor such a person, that meeting him we should destroy him — but first of all let us see him in ourselves, so that we can, in purity, unite ourselves with our national martyrs.

We don't want to suffer from the character of Brouček as we see the Russians suffer from their Oblomovs.

Such thoughts as these forced me to take up my pen to compose Mr Brouček's Excursions. The satire bites as if into living flesh, and my pen often paused.

Was the tone too soft, perhaps? Possibly not sharp

enough? Doesn't it pass over rather than judge? Does it excuse rather than condemn?

Isn't it the sweetness rather than the bitterness of truth that is revealed in him? Isn't there only goodness in him, rather than the violence of poison?

If the music seems rough, isn't it to confront us boldly with the truth? If this truth strips us, isn't it so that we burn with shame about ourselves? Is this biting satire enough to make us whip ourselves and the whole nation, or will it lull our conscience rather than awaken it?

The writings of Svatopluk Čech have scourged us — will the music add a serpent's tooth to his cat-o'-nine-tails?

With music, the colours of the pictures will glow so that they speak clearly, even to a simple mind, telling it not to be evasive, vain, humble, miserable, despicable.

The great day is coming nearer. It will smooth away the wrinkles of doubt, of weakness, mistrust and bondage on your brow. On your forehead will shine the star of hope.

These thoughts were the burning stimulus to work. The more terrible the situation, the more rapid the flow of ideas for composition.

Let the work spring to life, so that it may speak.

As for irony and sarcasm, how to find the right note? Think! There is nothing left on the moon for Brouček, but starvation. Secretly, he eats the last pair of sausages.

"He is eating, he is eating," shout the terrified Moon people, "Meat."

"I hope you don't think this is human flesh."

The Moon Ruler (pointing at the remainder of the sausage), "And is this a slaughtered animal?"

Brouček (furious):"Yes, pork, cut small and squeezed into gut, which....."

This is what you want to compose? You never will, you know! But, it will make a good news item for the papers.

Terrified of Professor Helfert, the merciless critic of Mr Brouček's expedition to the moon, I think of the catalogues of music literature.

What about words like ''God's day is upon us, and ''The Lord's day is coming''? I can easily do that, coming as I do from an organ school. It will be more difficult to do the Hussites of the 15th century because we already have from these ancient times Fibich's *Šărka*, Smetana's *Libuše*, and Doležel's collection of Hussite songs.

Eureka! Sometimes at the right momént comes the right idea.

It really has been hard work to translate the real-life excursions of Mr Brouček in depth, to change mere dreams into reality, to limit the poetically-minded to Mr Brouček's horizon. I had to unite *The Excursions* into a bi-ology (two operas, making a whole).

To obtain dramatic effect, the universe and the moon both had to be brought onto the stage as if by magical means.

The evening star had to be changed to a lantern on the corner of the Vikárka Inn. A complete somersault must transfer the whole company from the Dome of Art on the Moon to the front of the Vikárka Inn. The sun must rise over Prague on that memorable Sunday, 14th July 1420 for the burning of Brouček (symbol of Huss), and finish in 1888, to find Brouček in a barrel, at least a little ashamed of himself.

To the symposium created by Svatopluk Čech were added many ideas, variations, jokes, songs and caricatures by friends.

Jokingly, I could ask, as in the folk song

''Wait, stop and wait!

--------

Let us count,
If we are all here.''

Similarly it is said that Mrs Forester, before her birth, was an owl, and the wealthy landlord, the badger, is an analogy of the priest. The opposing elements in nature are the basis of Janáček's *Little Vixen*. The animals, insects, birds and plants have certain features in common with human nature, but on the other hand man has many animal characteristics inherited from the insects. It is as if there were neither absolute animals, nor absolute people.

The exception is the forester. He loves people as he also loves his forest and its inhabitants. He defends it against human beings whom he blames for damaging the forest. He is a bridge between people and animals.

Bystrouška brought to the forest instinctive hatred of humans and all that surrounds them. It seems that only with Lapák, the forester's dog, does she get on well. But Lapák is too denatured by human affairs and smells, and he confides in Bystrouška a lot of things he doesn't understand, mainly about love and art.

Out of her hatred the little *vixen* undertakes a treacherous fight. She acts politically, and with a rousing speech she incites the hens against the cock, saying that they should have an easier life. She behaves quite differently with animals in the wild — there she acts naturally. If she wants to evict the badger from his lair, she infuriates him by urinating there, so that he has to leave his home.

In the forester's enclosure she directly opposes everyone, while in the forest she lures the poacher with a trick, and then trips him up. She gets on well with the animals and all the inhabitants of the forest meet at her wedding. Birds, insects and squirrels enormously enjoy this festivity of humans and animals, but for safety the squirrels stay hopping about in the trees, while the woodpecker marries the foxes, and the turtledoves act as witnesses. A scene worthy of Noah's Ark!

The forester spares the vixen: Bystrouška falls not by his shot, but by the poacher's. She dies, but her little ones, the tiny little foxes, are safe and inherit the customs and manners of their mother. They know the forester through their mother, as do all the remaining youth of the forest. And when the forester has a little nap in the forest Bystrouška's cubs run around him; the little frog comes to see what is going on, and the tiniest little vixen, the exact image of her mother, runs and looks up into his face.

That evening I listened to Zitek's explanation: it rained in the forest. I have heard that the forest population often changes on the stage into living décor and with Bystrouška lives once more, so that she doesn't feel lonely; where she never dared to go before,there in the theatre where dreams and reality meet.

"To beat me, to kill me, just because I am a fox?", asks Bystrouška in Janáček's opera. I think of Hamlet, who of course was a Prince of Denmark, while she was from the lowest level of the animal world. Suddenly I feel like the forester when he promises himself, "I'll catch you, like your mother, but I shall educate you better, so that people won't write about you and me in the newspapers."

One more little word in farewell, my darling little daughter. Your mother's speech was the people's tongue, but you are educated and in moments of exaltation you speak almost like a lady. Well, we walk differently on the springy moss of the heath than we do on a well-trodden path. Be a joy to your foster-father who adopted you and send greetings to the world from hundreds and thousands of primroses and anemones which blossom and will blossom again.

1.11.1924.

## SONG OF THE FOX-CUBS

Janáček wrote this penny-polka for a collection of national dances and on a melody collected by Fr. Kyselková

## KRAJCPOLKA

*Sběratelka: Fr. Kyselková*        Leoš Janáček

Bratr umřel, já sem zustál,
já sem po něm boty dostál.

My brother died and I was left
Now I have his boots

17.2.1912

# FANFARE FOR THE NATIONAL GAMES OF 1926

## SLETOVÉ FANFÁRY

### Leoše Janáčka

The victorious mood of this fanfare has the same optimism as the opening fanfares of the *Sinfonietta* written a year later

V.T.